Colin Ward was born in 1924 was Editor of *Anarchy* throughout the 1960s and of the *Bulletin of Environmental Action* throughout the 1970s. He is the author of *Anarchy in Action* (Allen & Unwin), *Vandalism* (Architectural Press), *Tenants Take Over* (Architectural Press), *Housing: An Anarchist Approach* (Freedom Press) and *The Child in the City* (Penguin). With Anthony Fyson he wrote *Streetwork: the Exploding School* (Routledge & Kegan Paul), with Eileen Adams, *Art and the Built Environment* (Longman) and with Dennis Hardy, *Arcadia for All* (Mansell). He contributes regularly to *New Society*.

Colin Ward

When We Build Again

Let's Have Housing that Works!

Pluto Press
London and Sydney

First published in 1985 by Pluto Press Limited,
The Works, 105a Torriano Avenue, London NW5 2RX
and Pluto Press Australia Limited, PO Box 199, Leichhardt,
New South Wales 2040, Australia

Copyright © Colin Ward 1985

Typeset by Photobooks (Bristol) Limited
Printed in Great Britain by Guernsey Press Co. Limited,
Guernsey, C.I.

British Library Cataloguing in Publication Data
Ward, Colin
    When we build again: Let's have housing that works!
    1. Housing——Great Britain
    I. Title
    363.5'0941   HD7333.A

ISBN 0 7453 0022 7

Contents

Acknowledgements / 7

Preface / 9

1. Where we went wrong / 11
2. Self-help and mutual aid: the stolen vocabulary / 27
3. Is selling off a sell-out? / 46
4. Learning from the poor / 57
5. Plots of freedom / 71
6. Rediscovering co-operation / 85
7. Leavening the Lump / 99
8. Do we need a plan? / 109

Notes / 121

Acknowledgements

Parts of Chapter 1 and other fragments of this text were originally published in the 'Stand' column of *New Society* and I am grateful to the editor for the hospitality of his pages and for permission to reprint. Chapter 2 is based on my contribution to a book commissioned but never published by the Architectural Press (*Participation in Housing*, edited by Nabeel Hamdi). Chapter 3 is based on my contribution to *Emergency*, No. 2, 1984.

Preface

I have borrowed the title of this little book from that of one of the many wartime publications on the theme of postwar reconstruction. *When We Build Again* was produced in 1941 by the Bourneville Village Trust and envisaged a Britain rebuilt in the image of Ebenezer Howard's two garden cities, Letchworth and Welwyn. It didn't happen that way. The wartime moratorium on house building provided an opportunity for reformulating housing policy, learning from the mistakes of the past. But we didn't. Forty-four years after *When We Build Again*, after an immense public investment in housing, we are in another moratorium, and it would be misleading to call it the Thatcher moratorium because already by 1973 we were lamenting the fact that public investment in housing was lower than in any previous postwar year. But we are *not* using the moratorium to think again about the fundamentals of housing policy, even though, as the architect Nick Wates puts it, 'the painful realization that housing policy has been a key cause of the Labour Party's downfall is beginning to sink in.'[1]

A glance in the window of any estate agent in any high street shows that we don't have a housing shortage, just a poverty problem. But this book is not about the abolition of poverty or the abolition of capitalism, neither of which is likely in our lifetimes. It is about the capacity of poor people to house themselves if helped rather than hindered. For generations of socialists in and out of office, this has seemed totally irrelevant: massive programmes of planned government expenditure were the obvious way of coping with housing needs; technology, professionalism and large-scale industry would do the job. But the introduction to a recent volume on urban history[2] contains the terse little comment that 'having demolished slums which stood for a century, we constructed homes which lasted a decade.' Unfair? Untrue? Most people in most British cities will readily think of examples. The authors declare that 'damp, boredom, vandalism and garbage undermined the urban vision'. But another factor needs pondering. Housing policy assumes that people are helpless and inert consumers and ignores their ability and their yearnings to shape their own environment. We are paying today for confusing paternalistic authoritarianism with socialism and social responsibility. When we build again, let's give people a chance and have housing that works!

1. Where we went wrong

> Mass Housing in its original conception was never intended to house the entire community. It was merely an emergency measure which was seized upon when the normal process fell short. It was a means which was useful when large numbers of people had to be housed in a short space of time. It was used when for various reasons the natural relationship had already been interrupted, and when certain groups of people for one reason or another could not house themselves – groups which were originally housed in this way were paupers just because they had no place in the normal pattern; because they had become isolated from it; and had to be housed by an external pressure, by an artificial effort. Mass Housing has indeed been a blessing in recent times for countless people, and as an emergency measure has contributed to the fact that our civilization has survived the industrial revolution. *But our problem began when this emergency measure from the turn of the century grew into housing for the entire community, and thus became the norm.*
>
> N.J. Habraken, *Supports: an Alternative to Mass Housing*, 1972.

My youngest child wanted to know why there were modern houses in a derelict state in our local small town. I asked him what street they were in, though of course I knew, just as you automatically have guessed, that they must be houses owned by the local authority. So I explained that the wicked Secretary of State for the Environment had denied Babergh District Council the cash to repair them, and indeed was (as an ultimate betrayal of the working class, etc.) urging the council to sell the ones next door to their occupiers.

'But weren't you moaning the other day that the council has just spent £2¾ million pounds on its new offices?' 'That's different,' I replied. 'Why?' he persisted. For he had probably seen the demonstration when the new offices were opened, when 'Council tenants whose homes still have outside toilets, stood for over an hour in the pouring rain protesting outside Babergh's palatial new offices at Hadleigh.'[1] Of course the council's Housing Services Officer explained that 'there was no relation between the new headquarters and money available for modernizing council houses.'

Now I like the new council offices. They form a lovely group of buildings and I rejoice that the hundred staff members have delightful working conditions at a cost of £27,500 each. But I also feel a certain responsibility towards the council's tenants and their living conditions. Twelve years ago, when a city dweller, I wrote a book called *Tenants Take Over*, which, so I thought, offered a creative solution for the dilemmas of local authority housing. When I described the humiliating paternalism of councils' approach to their tenants, people in the housing world told me, firstly, that my criticisms were out of date, and secondly, that I was generalizing from the experience of the hard-pressed inner cities. In the country everything was different. On the first of these points, I find my misgivings confirmed by the commendably frank account by a life-long socialist, Tony Judge, of his experience as Chair of the Housing Management Committee of the Greater London Council from 1974 to 1977. He says that 'The impression, often confirmed as accurate on deeper examination, is of a vast bureaucracy concerned more with self-perpetuation than with either efficiency or humanity', and he bitterly criticizes 'the insufferably paternalistic attitudes of councils and officials to their tenants'.[2]

On the second point, I have since moved to the country, to relatively prosperous East Anglia. Even my children notice the paradox of derelict modern houses, and even here we have demonstrations by tenants who feel outraged by their neglect by the well-housed council officers. The tenant spokesperson, Raymond Briggs, who spent £1,000 on modernizing the kitchen of the council house in Guthrum Road which he has rented since it was built 30 years ago, described the council's continually postponed promises, and explained that 'Most of the houses have still got old sinks and no heating. The doors don't fit properly and the houses are cold and damp. They want our rent but are not prepared to do anything to these houses. Last year they increased the rents by 17 per cent but still say there is no money to provide inside toilets.'[3]

Children like simple explanations, and it wasn't easy for me to explain to my son why, blinded by ideology and ignoring observable facts, we have been so brainwashed as to equate local-authority landlordism with a socialist approach to housing. What I was tempted to say was that those houses had been *decommodified*, thus giving a new twist to a concept I have learned from the academics of housing. In 1981 Michael Harloe wrote a paper defining the sale of council houses to sitting tenants as 'the recommodification of housing'[4] and in the following year he had the temerity to barge in on one of those ludicrous polemics among Marxist pundits with a comment called 'Towards the Decommodification of Housing' in which, trying hard to bring a little common sense into the discussion, he argued that 'socialized housing need not imply an attack on the individual ownership of housing, it does imply an attack on the provision of housing as a commodity whether it be owned or rented.'[5] When I adopt his phraseology for a different purpose, I am simply using an older meaning of the word commodity. Sir

Henry Wootton, 350 years ago, said that a house must have 'commoditie, firmness and delight', meaning that it must have usefulness and convenience as well as those other essential attributes. The unique achievement of our system of public housing provision has indeed been to decommodify housing by turning it from a social asset to a social liability. This explains the reluctance of the London boroughs to take over the GLC's housing, as provided for years ago in the London Government Act of 1963, just as it explains the refusal of some local authorities in new town areas to take over the new town housing on the winding up of the development corporations. The people who drafted the legislation could not envisage that all the huge public investment and expensive architectural expertise represented by GLC and new town housing, would be a headache, rather than a godsend, to the local council's housing committees and officers.

Scarcely a week goes by without the press reporting that yet another council has decided to decommodify its tower blocks, which it won't have finished paying for for another 50 years, in the most literal way, by paying a demolition contractor large sums to pull them down or blow them up. They are throwing away, remember, not only the continuing subsidy, and the potential rent or sale income, but a huge area of covered space, which, when you consider the current cost of building *anything* could surely be useful for *something*.

If there was a branch of social science called the psychology of public accountability, it might explain the determination to decommodify by removing past errors from the face of the earth, or just to be rid of administrative embarrassments. In the period leading up to the eventual demolition in 1979 of Oak and Eldon Gardens, Birkenhead, I spoke to everyone concerned, from council officers to the then MP for the area, urging that some effort should be made to sell them to a private buyer, but they all agreed that no-one in their senses would want to live there. Had they waited a few years, Sir

Lawrie Barratt would have been there in his helicopter to make a bid.

A press interview with Barratt describes his deal with Liverpool corporation to buy, not tower blocks, but 46-year-old flats at £1,000 a unit, refurbish them and then 'market them at a far lower cost than people would normally have to pay for two bedroom flats'. He 'reeled off' to Michael Dineen, 'statistics of thousands of council properties, many only a dozen years old, which have either been demolished or are awaiting the arrival of the bulldozer. In the London borough of Hillingdon, 1,185; Spennymoor, County Durham, 560 (only 13 years old); Manchester, 1,018; and a further 3,000 divided between council estates in Hull, Leeds, Nottingham and Sheffield.'[6]

You don't have to be in love with the Barratt organization to see the force of his argument. The recommodification of housing which has been decommodified in this sense is undoubtedly a social good. It houses someone and it makes something useful out of the human labour and investment that the building represents. When David Alton, as Chair of Liverpool Housing Committee, said he would accept *any* offer for the so-called Everton piggeries as an alternative to hiring someone to blow them up, he was talking sense. The council put the blocks out to tender for a peppercorn fee of £1 'in the belief that the cleared site would be worth less than the cost of demolition' and they were finally sold for conversion into 373 flats for a total of £51,000 to include £1,000 for the lease and £250 for every flat sold.[7] The sum may be pathetic by comparison with the council's investment, but it does make the best of a bad job.

Edinburgh council, faced with the desirability of demolishing Martello Court, was urged to sell the building off in the private market, and sold it to a developer for £200,000. The purchaser spent another £400,000 on turning the flats into owner-occupied dwellings. When I took some students to see this bit of recommodification, an island in a sea of municipal demolition, we couldn't get past the perimeter wall. Quite right too, I thought. It is only council tenants who are regarded as fair game for sociological voyeurism. We learned that the residents are first-time buyers, paying about £10,000 with mortgages.

On the other hand, Glasgow council has swallowed its pride and promoted an experiment in urban homesteading at Easterhouse. This estate, which was subjected to a malevolent media amplification of its juvenile problems back in the 1960s, has been in a state of decommodification ever since. But in 1981 freeholds in a few of its empty three-storey walk-up blocks were offered, together with a grant for rehabilitation, to families willing to take them on, and the experiment hasn't made news because it has worked.

Alison Ravetz, author of a housing classic which chronicled the rise and fall of the famous Leeds estate Quarry Hill (where, when after decades of travail the residents had finally made a workable community, the council decided to demolish without any reference to them), recently remarked that 'the life of council estates gets shorter all the time'.[8] She was commenting on Leeds council's decision in June 1982 to demolish, at a cost of £400,000, all the 1,249 flats at Hunslet Grange, with outstanding debt charges of £4.7 million. In her view, not the least of the tragedies of this adventure was the 'wilful refusal to listen to people who know their own environment.' History repeats itself, said Marx, first as tragedy, than as farce. The farce happened in the same month as the Leeds decision, when in a triumph of decommodification 23 families were made homeless at Kirby. In one of those spectacular municipal blow-ups, five blocks of flats, built in 1970, were demolished in an explosion which also demolished uncondemned housing nearby. More traditional means of demolition are to be used for decommodifying the rest of the £6 million estate, and the *Architects' Journal* commented that this experience 'may have put an end to the present vogue for blowing up council flats.'

Not since Chancellor Dollfuss trained his artillery on the Karl Marx Hof in Vienna in 1934 has there been such an assault upon public investment in housing. And apart from the local authorities' determination to destroy public property, there were by 1981 over 135,000 empty council dwellings in England and Wales, and over a quarter of a million classified as 'hard to let'. I am desolated, if unsurprised, by the response not just of the politicians, who undoubtedly recognize that patronage in the form of housing is power, but also of the academics and 'experts' who, spared the anguish of day-to-day contact with outraged tenants or helpless supplicants, might be expected to have a more detached approach to our housing dilemmas.

But when in the journal *Critical Social Policy*, Sidney Jacobs dared to ask, 'The sale of council houses: does it matter?' he was soundly trounced by those who thought it did. He dared to condemn the attitude pressed on local government officers by the authors of the pamphlet 'The Great Sales Robbery'. He states,

> their tactics are designed to delay, frustrate and ultimately to undermine individual attempts to buy council houses and, short of organizing pogroms against prospective buyers, it would be difficult to devise a strategy more certain to individualize, personalize and alienate. For instance, local authorities are advised to 'ensure the highest possible valuation for each dwelling'; 'refuse to finalize completion of a sale . . . until forced to do so by the tenant obtaining an injunction'; 'ensure high service charges as a deterrent to those buying flats'; and so forth. It seems that, in the name of protecting working-class housing, the opponents of sales intend to inflict upon workers who want to buy their council houses the kind of treatment which in other circumstances they would be among the first to denounce as bureaucratic despotism.[9]

In a nation where over 50 or perhaps nearer 60 per cent of households are in owner-occupation, there is a kind of electoral unwisdom in the reluctance to help people get out from under municipal patronage and continual rent rises which bear no relation to economic rents or historic costs, into the kind of tenure taken for granted by the majority of their fellow citizens. But this is not my business. What does concern me is finding strategies to halt the social irresponsibility of decommodifying housing. Why is it that on one side of the street the council is demolishing old houses as unfit for human habitation and replacing them by flats which nobody likes (and will be pulled down long before the houses opposite), while on the other side of the street, identical houses are being bought and improved by those despised gentrifiers, and given an indefinite new life? Why is it that on one side of town the speculative builder's sub-Parker Morris houses are enhanced from the moment they are occupied, while on the other side of the town, the high-quality council development declines from the time the tenants move in? I have been asking these questions, on the platform and in print, for well over a decade but nobody has thought them worth answering.

The answer doesn't lie in the mystique or even the direct financial advantage of ownership as such. After all, the tenants who pay their rent regularly, and don't join the ranks of those known in Glasgow as 'corporation cast-offs', have a lifetime tenure too, which is all the owner-occupier can claim. The difference relates to the situation they find themselves in – the fact that some people have a vested interest in the survival of the estate and are in control of their own environment.

If dweller control were accepted as the first principle of housing policy, most of those unlettable or hard-to-let flats would never have been built in the first place; but if it were adopted as the rule rather than the exception, the cycle of decline into decommodification could be arrested. To find what went wrong we have to ask the question: 'Where did we go wrong?' and the answer is to be found not in the technology but in the psychology of housing.

Three human needs – food, clothing and shelter – are so fundamental that our life cannot continue without them. It is humbling to think of the tenacity and ingenuity with which our forebears survived, feeding, clothing and housing themselves from the materials that their environment provided even in desert or arctic wastes. They didn't do it in lonely isolation. They worked together in families, tribes, village communities. In modern governmental societies the division of people into haves and have-nots ensures that it is possible to starve in the richest country in the world, just as it is possible to live in luxury in the poorest. But these are extremes. Most of the world's people feed, clothe and house themselves, usually in co-operation with their neighbours, sometimes with the help of their rulers, sometimes despite them, and take some pleasure in doing so. In most countries government assumes some responsibility for providing basic needs if people are unable to meet them themselves. Whether this is described as social responsibility, charity, welfare or the process of capitalist reproduction depends upon your point of view.

When in times of scarcity government provides the basic necessities of life, through, for example, a rationing system in times of war or natural disaster, we call it a siege economy; when it is a matter of governmentally imposed economic priorities, a command economy. But because people have a natural urge to feed, clothe and house themselves and their families, they have a tendency to despise the official provision, to circumvent it if possible, and certainly to improve upon it. They actually *prefer* the results of their own initiative, the alternative or the improvised, even though it may be inferior to that which is officially provided.

Consider Britain in a period of siege economy: The Second World War. Food policy ensured a nutritionally better diet than poor people were able to obtain in the prewar years. The wartime national loaf was better than the white bread in the baker's shop before or since. Wartime children's teeth were better than those of the earlier or later generation, because of the limited sugar in their diet. Yet when food rationing was finally abandoned, seven years after the war, people rejoiced in being able to eat what they liked. The Conservative Party was able to campaign in the election of 1951 under the slogan of Lord Woolton, the wartime food controller, 'More Red Meat'. And they won. Institutional catering was and is always disparaged by its recipients, 'utility' clothing and 'utility' furniture was equally devalued, even though the furniture was designed by a renowned maker, Gordon Russell, and was of a far higher standard of construction than the normal products of the industry. Honourable words like 'utility' and 'austerity' became labels of disdain and contempt. Sad to say, though the direct public provision of housing for rent was not just a matter of wartime or postwar emergencies, but is much longer established in British life, it is subject to the same undervaluation. What is the highest praise that a local authority tenant can give to his or her house? 'It doesn't look like a council house.'

Over 20 years ago, the Dutch architect, Nicholas John Habraken, wrote a book which is a sustained criticism of the philosophy of what he calls MH – mass housing. Habraken remarks,

> It is one of the wonders of our existence that the satisfaction of some requirements demands a very positive, personal, almost creative action on our part. Even today no-one would maintain that we can live merely by consumption, no matter how attractively or skilfully consumer goods are presented. *But Mass Housing reduces the dwelling to a consumer article and the dweller to a consumer. For only in this way can it be expected that the consumer waits until he is offered a*

completed product. It need not surprise us if this approach proves wrong because individual human action forms part of the housing brief.[10]

It is time, Habraken declares, 'to break the bonds of Mass Housing, and at least to inquire what the individual can contribute to the housing process', something which, the policies of Mass Housing deny *a priori* and leave out of the discussion of housing policy. 'Mass Housing pretends that the involvement of the individual and all that it implies simply ought not to exist. The provision of housing therefore cannot be called a process of man housing himself. Man no longer houses himself: he is housed.'

Habraken does of course have a selective view of history: if they were poor, our European ancestors of say the seventeenth or eighteenth centuries, lived in shanties of mud and straw, not a trace of which now remains. The vernacular architecture we have all learned to love housed the superior artisan class rather than the poor of preindustrial society; and the industrial poor of the nineteenth century lived in grossly overcrowded slums. All they contributed to the housing process was rent.

But Habraken is voicing an aspiration that runs very deep. Here are two passages from famous writers from the middle of the last century, lamenting the alienation of the dweller from the dwelling:

1. In the large towns and cities where civilization especially prevails, the number of those who can own a shelter is a very small fraction of the whole. The rest pay an annual tax for this outside garment of all, become indispensable summer and winter, which would buy a village of Indian wigwams, but now helps to keep them poor as long as they live . . . On the one side is the palace, on the other are the almshouse and 'silent poor'. The myriads who built the pyramids to be the tombs of the Pharoahs were fed on garlic, and

it may be were not decently buried themselves. The mason who finishes the cornice of the palace returns at night perchance to a hut not so good as a wigwam. It is a mistake to suppose that, in a country where the usual evidences of civilization exist, the conditions of a very large body of the inhabitants may not be as degraded as that of savages.

2. Man is regressing to the cave dwelling, but in an alienated, malignant form. The savage in his cave (a natural element which is freely offered for his use and protection) does not feel himself a stranger; on the contrary he feels as much at home as a fish in water. But the cellar dwelling of the poor man is a hostile dwelling, 'an alien, constricting power which only surrenders itself to him in exchange for blood and sweat.' He cannot regard it as his home, as a place where he might at last say, 'here I am at home.' Instead, he finds himself in *another person's* house, the house of a *stranger* who lies in wait for him every day and evicts him if he does not pay the rent.

I owe this remarkable parallel to Professor Staughton Lynd, who invites readers to guess which of these passages comes from Karl Marx and which from Henry David Thoreau, writing from the hut he built by Walden Pond.[11]

The tragedy of public involvement in the provision of housing, and many of the difficulties and paradoxes it has brought us, lies precisely in the fact that it has not changed this alienation of the dweller from the dwelling. As Habraken remarks in the passage I quote at the start of this chapter, 'our problem began when this emergency measure from the turn of the century grew into housing for the entire community, and thus became the norm.' Actually it only became the norm, in his country and ours, for those people who could not or did not escape from landlordism into owner-occupation.

The revolution in house tenure in this century has been far more significant than the revolution in building techniques or in the standards of servicing in housing. Until the end of the First World War, 90 per cent of households, rich or poor, rented their accommodation from a private landlord. Today, although the proportion differs in different parts of the country, well over half all households in Britain live in owner-occupied dwellings. Another third have as their landlords local authorities, and the privately rented sector continually dwindles. This change towards owner-occupation has profoundly affected the esteem in which housing is held by its occupants, and it also (since all British governments depend on the marginal voter in the marginal owner-occupied constituency) strongly influences the policies of those who find themselves in office.

Slowly and tentatively, at the end of the last century, government and local authorities began to take over the role of the private landlord. After the efforts of philanthropists to demonstrate that slums could be replaced by model dwellings for the industrial classes and still yield a return on capital of 4 or 5 per cent, the conclusion was reached that this was a task for councils. There was a kind of political consensus on this point that linked Fabian socialists in the infant London County Council with their belief in 'gas and water socialism' and radical politicians – Liberal, Liberal-Unionist or Conservative, like Joseph Chamberlain in Birmingham.

What began as a measure to replace the inner-city warrens and rookeries swept away by road improvements, sewerage schemes and slum clearance, to the benefit of the new tenants (who were not usually the displaced former inhabitants who could neither afford the rents nor accommodate themselves to the atmosphere of social improvement), became a general aspiration to replace working-class housing.

The First World War with its housing shortage and its mood of resolution to build a land fit for heroes to live in, led to the Tudor Walters Report of 1918 with its detailed proposals for local authority house building, and to large-scale public provision for housing between the wars. In the Second World War the prospect of a greater housing shortage and the same aspiration for change led to local authority housing being part of the progressive creed among all parties. It was regarded as a great triumph in the housing legislation of the postwar government that the phrase 'housing of the working classes' disappeared from the wording of the Act, so that publicly provided housing for rent became a service for which, theoretically, the whole population was eligible. It is noticeable that those whose incomes or expectations gave them any freedom of choice, did not often take up this hypothetical option.

Local authority tenants have seldom been allowed to forget the missionary aspect of the origins of state housing provision. Beatrice Webb, immensely influential in the development of the Fabian approach to housing noted in her diary in 1885,

> To study state interference in its two separate functions is the special question: first of enforcing respect in the individual for the health of others, obliging the individual to fulfil the acknowledged contract with society; and secondly that more doubtfully natural function – its attempt to supplement by direct constructive activity the work of voluntary enterprise and of individual effort . . .[12]

The first intention was thus to teach sanitary habits to the deserving poor, and it is sobering to reflect that a century later the militant Marxist NALGO activists of housing management, whether they have convinced themselves that housing is simply an aspect of the process of capitalist reproduction or part of 'the social wage', are the same old Lady Bountifuls in their workaday activities.

Frank Field, Labour MP for Birkenhead, remarks that

Council tenants all too often live under a form of serfdom which takes on a number of forms. It limits a tenant's ability to move from one area to another, and it hems their lives with petty rules and restrictions. It has always puzzled me why owners on a Wimpey-type estate need no-one to tell them how to live, while the lives of council tenants are hedged around with rules and regulations which would hardly make sense even if the whole population was mentally handicapped.[13]

He was urging a change in his party's attitude to the sale of council houses to tenants, a change which he thought would be welcome in a party 'that has got into the habit of refusing to listen to its supporters.' I don't know how long it will take to convince socialists that their beliefs are seen by ordinary citizens as just another excuse for bureaucracy pushing people around for their own good, but I would like to draw their attention to another sentence in Beatrice Webb's diary in 1885, *a century ago*. She remarked, 'The idea of developing self-government among the tenants has to be gradually introduced.'

So gradual has been this introduction, that 100 years later you can count on one hand the number of councils who have made the slightest gesture towards dweller self-government. I was present myself at a meeting to discuss one councillor's very mild proposals for tenant involvement in housing management in a north London borough, when the outraged representative of one of the local government unions got to his feet and said, 'We're not going to be dictated to by a bunch of tenants.'

Raymond Unwin, the architect of the Tudor Walters report which, after the First World War, set the pattern for local authority landlordism ever since, was in fact an earnest advocate of housing co-operatives. There is a sad paradox that the original inspirers of the direct provision of housing by local authorities saw it as a necessary step towards a more desirable mode of tenure. That step was never taken. What began as 'an emergency measure from the turn of the century' became institutionalized as virtually the only alternative to house purchase.

2. Self-help and mutual aid: the stolen vocabulary

'Private faces in public places
Are wiser and nicer
Than public faces in private places'
W.H. Auden, *Marginalia*.

The most depressing thing about the ideological mess we have made for ourselves in the field of housing is that whenever someone on a public platform eulogizes self-help and mutual aid, half the audience stop listening since they regard these words not merely as Conservative platitudes but as a smokescreen to conceal the abdication of governmental responsibilities. I cannot imagine how these phrases came to be dirty words for socialists since they refer to human attributes without which any conceivable socialist society would founder.

Nor are they part of the official perception of housing policy. The Department of the Environment in its towers at Marsham Street has a vast library. You could, if you were admitted, go there and read the entire official literature of housing, from the 1880s to the 1970s, and you would not find either phrase. They have never been on the agenda in the language of government.

They are resonant phrases because both are the titles of famous books from the Victorian era. *Mutual Aid* by the Russian anarchist, Peter Kropotkin, was a celebration of the propensity to co-operate, whether among insects, animals or humans, intended as a rebuttal of the misinterpretations by

Thomas Henry Huxley and Alfred Russell Wallace of the implications of Darwin's theory of natural selection.

Self-Help by Samuel Smiles was a much-reprinted volume which exhorted its readers to apply thrift and self-improvement to their lives so as to progress from rags to riches. Smiles himself was outraged that his book had been regarded as a manual on devil-take-the-hindmost individualism, declaring in the Preface to the second edition that this was 'the very opposite of what it really is . . . Although its chief object unquestionably is to stimulate youths to rely upon their own efforts in life rather than depend upon the help or patronage of others, it will also be found . . . that the duty of helping one's self in the highest sense involves the helping of one's neighbours.'

Our ancestors were kept alive only by a combination of self-help and mutual aid, and this was the dominant characteristic of the emerging working-class organizations of the nineteenth century, whether we are thinking of the cooperative movement, the trade union movement, the friendly society movement or the adult education movement. It is ironical that the twentieth-century political heirs of these organizations have put their faith exclusively in the governmental bureaucracy and have not only ignored this heritage, but despise it.

Interestingly enough, until the revival of interest in the late 1960s in the application of mutual aid and self-help to housing, it was only among immigrant groups in Britain, whose whole experience of the role of government in their lives predisposes them towards non-governmental solutions, that you could find the modern equivalent of the very earliest building societies. Thus the Milner Holland Report on housing in London noted that,

> Particularly among Indians and Pakistanis, housing finance pools are found with a substantial membership – perhaps as many as 900 – which meet periodically

once a fortnight or once a month, and make calls of,
say, £10 on each member. Those who draw upon the
fund thus created are subject thereafter to periodic
calls until the whole amount drawn by them has been
liquidated. Drawings under this system are substantial
and may cover the whole purchase cost. Occasionally
West Indians operate on similar but less ambitious
lines . . . Their pooling arrangements usually only
provide for the initial deposits necessary for house
purchase, thus enabling them to 'get off the ground'.[1]

Of course, the whole owner-occupation sector in housing is, though it is very unfashionable to say so except in Conservative circles, a triumphant example of self-help and mutual aid. Building societies originated as working-class organizations; they are by definition and by law non-profit-making bodies, even though the vain attempts by ordinary members to get elected to their boards may persuade us that they are ruled, like many other organizations with similar origins, by self-perpetuating oligarchies.

One could even make a case, historically, for the notion that the first building societies were formed when as a result of the enclosures, squatters or cottagers (two terms which were once synonymous) were no longer able to erect their dwellings on waste or common land. Not only in Britain, but in many parts of Europe, and hence in the New World, it became widely accepted that if a person succeeded in erecting a dwelling between sunset and sunrise and lighting a fire in it, he or she could not lawfully be dispossessed. There are innumerable variations on this formula – six months, a year and a day, twelve years – in which property might be occupied unchallenged to gain title, whether enshrined in folk law, common law or even statute law.

Observers noted how the hovels of the peasantry could develop over generations into a fully finished house. For William Cobbett, the cottager was a free and independent spirit saved from the craven poverty of the landless labourer. An account of the squatters of the New Forest stresses their prosperity and self-sufficiency, and their 'singular combination of reticence and self-possession, with good humour and friendliness.'[2] To relate personality characteristics to the mode of tenure is a risky argument since so many factors quite outside the control of the individual shape our lives and life-chances. But such generalizations are still made. When Ferdynand Zweig asked people how they felt when they became house owners, 'the overwhelming majority felt deeply about it' and the words which came to their lips were 'satisfaction, self-confidence, freedom and independence.'[3]

In his study of the history of working-class housing in Nottingham, Stanley Chapman notes that as late as 1785 just a few industrious artisans were to be found building their own cottages. He cites the case of William Felkin, a knitter in the hosiery trade, an abstemious man engaged on the highest-quality work, who was 38 before he was able to build his own cottage. He was granted a plot, 60 yards by 10 yards, by the squire of the village of Bramcote, and with the aid of his son, built his cottage of brick, stone, timber and thatch.

> The dwelling house, consisting of house place and weaving shop, scullery, pantry, and with two bedrooms above, was 32 feet long and 16 feet in width, and the height of the roof tree was 26 feet, the roof thatched or tiled. Adjoining was a building open to the roof, furnished with a large bread oven, copper and space for coal and firewood. Another lean-to was for a piggery and hen roost . . . The garden space was 450 square yards.[4]

For most working men this was a dream rather than a reality, but as enclosures and urbanization created the industrial proletariat, various mutual aid institutions grew up among people who wanted to free themselves from landlords and rent. Chapman finds traces of the existence in Nottingham of working-class 'money clubs' for the raising of capital to enable builders to erect small houses for club members. Borrowing from these money clubs seems, he says, to represent a transition between the friendly society and the 'terminating' building society. In another paper he examines such institutions in Birmingham in the late eighteenth and early nineteenth centuries. Two kinds of societies were organized, from below, to serve as the mechanisms of both self-help and mutual aid in housing. The terminating building societies (so named to distinguish them from the permanent building societies which superseded them) were formed by groups of people who pooled their creditworthiness to build a group of houses which, when completed, were allocated to members of the group. Freehold land societies, with a similar aim, acquired land for subdivision into plots for their members. One of the motives of the Freehold Land Society in Birmingham in the mid-nineteenth century was also that of providing the property qualification for the parliamentary vote, and in the words of Chapman and Bartlett, it 'was quickly taken over by the artisan elite and small manufacturers.'[5]

The incomes of the poor were so low and their insecurity so manifest, that the capacity for regular saving through any such societies did not apply to them. But between the appalling housing conditions of the 'submerged tenth' and the propensity for self-help and mutual aid of the highly skilled artisan class, there were families living in rented houses in the long terraces of the familiar 'by-law' streets built between, say, 1875 and 1914. Our impression of such streets may very well be one of 'dirty brick or stonework, rusting metalwork, and unpainted timber', but Francis Jones reminds us that 'prior to 1914 the renting of a house was an economically sound policy, and maintenance, however it was organized, was essential to the landlord.' And the tenants' part in the process? Jones remarks that,

In addition to the standard of landlord maintenance the tenants had common standards for the exterior of the house. This included sweeping the pavement and often even mopping it for the full width of the house. The window-sills were painted and polished, doorsteps were rubbed clean and colourwashed white or buff. Metal door furniture was either directly polished if brass or black-polished if cast-iron. The external woodwork, i.e. of door and lower windows, was washed regularly and polished. Through the windows clean curtains and shining metallic fittings would be visible. The general visual quality of the street was therefore bright, and even in streets consisting entirely of houses, uniformity did not necessarily mean a deadening monotony.[6]

After the slow decline in the interwar years, accelerating in the postwar period, this tradition of tenant involvement in maintenance became eroded as landlords themselves were unable or unwilling to meet their own maintenance obligations. What was the point in polishing the front door when the roof leaked? Today, if we see a house in a terraced street of this kind, treated with the sort of loving care that Mr Jones describes, we know that it has been purchased freehold by the occupier (in spite of the discrimination of most of the building societies against loans for this kind of house), or has been taken over by a tenants' co-operative.

The little Buckinghamshire town of Wolverton exemplifies this point dramatically. It grew up in the railway boom of the last century, with the district called New Bradwell being built by the railway company to house the people employed in the railway workshops in streets of little terrace houses characteristic of any industrial town. By the 1950s the local council, dominated by retired railway workers, saw this housing as mean and obsolete, redolent of the bad old days of nineteenth-century capitalism. Several streets were demolished and on their sites were built blocks of three-storey municpal flats, neither better nor worse than those of any other local authority. By the 1970s it had become evident that many people actually preferred the old streets to the new blocks, and there was fierce local argument about the wisdom of demolition. Finally, thanks to the sympathetic attention of members of the staff of Milton Keynes Development Corporation, the very oldest of the railway cottages (by now, such is the capriciousness of the cycle of taste, regarded as a little gem of nineteenth-century industrial architecture) were rehabilitated for the Rainbow Housing Co-operative which leased them collectively from the Corporation. They are now seen as the most attractive and desirable houses in the whole town.

When I asked a co-operative member there what the adventure meant for him, he replied,

> Well, we're in a position where we have more control over the houses that we're living in, how to decorate them, the way we'd like the street to look. There's more interest, more involvement and this provides a sort of common thread that runs through the street, and everybody knows everybody as a result through this common interest in running the place. It creates a very friendly atmosphere.

But so tortuously complex have we made the procedures for improvement grants and the establishment of co-operatives that this venture could never have got off the ground had it not been for the lucky accident that the Development Corporation staff's professional expertise was available. I say this not to praise the professionals, but to deplore the complexity of the legislation.

Another example of this deployment of self-help and mutual aid, which, however, was only brought about through the lucky accident of professional presence, is that of the Black Road, Macclesfield (a town in Cheshire which had played an important part in the early silk-weaving industry). The houses in this street, built around 1815, were originally scheduled for demolition in 1968. An architect, Rod Hackney, bought one of the houses towards the end of 1971 and applied for the standard improvement grant. The council turned down his application, as his 'structurally unsound' cottage was in the clearance area. When he wrote to the *Macclesfield Express* complaining of 'official vandalism' he found that many of his neighbours were in the the same situation and of the same mind, and inevitably he became both their spokesperson and their architect. The rest of the story is very well-known in housing circles and made the architect's reputation.

Black Road has certain special features which make it the archetypical example of self-help and mutual aid in housing renovation. It became, for instance, the first general improvement area in the country to be proposed, implemented and subsequently managed by the residents themselves. It was also the first example of that supreme irony of the crudity of official designations of places: of a clearance area being transformed into a conservation area. From being worthless the houses became priceless.

The Black Road Action Group succeeded in winning over the council's officers so that the rules could be relaxed in a most sensible way. For example, the rules specify that self-help is penalized in the sense that the dweller's own labour cannot qualify for grant. The authorities would rather pay a firm of building contractors than pay you or recognize your contribution. At Black Road neighbours set up as contractors for each other, so that they might qualify for grant aid. Poor and elderly tenants were enabled to become owner-occupiers, again just to qualify, through what Hackney calls Robin Hood financial arrangements, and each tenant got the improvements actually wanted, rather than those which the regulations or the architect thought was good for them, so that no two houses are by now alike. This marvellously intimate approach to the creative adventure of house improvement is symbolized by the fact that the building workers left their plant on Friday night at the most convenient places for the residents to take it over at the weekends.

Once again, the sad truth is that just because of the mountain of legislation and regulations, and just because it was necessary to have someone to put the case convincingly to the holders of power and dispensers of funds – a power of life and death over a street – it was essential to have someone present with professional knowledge and a vested interest in the success of the project. This in no way diminishes the potential of self-help and mutual aid. It simply demonstrates the extent to which the procedures introduced by government to improve the housing situation have unwittingly complicated it and made it unresponsive to the aspirations of ordinary citizens. The habit of self-help and mutual aid have been deliberately repressed by inducing the habit of reliance on the bureaucratic organization of housing. To paraphrase Habraken again, people are no longer enabled to house themselves: they have to rely on being housed.

Not only that: they are expected to be grateful and to stay put. For one aspect of the demise of the private landlord which nobody ever mentions is the loss of the freedom to move. The public sector is the immobile sector, and owner-occupiers, with the millstone of mortgages round their necks are more mobile than council tenants, dependent upon the goodwill of the clerks in the housing department. Our views on the historical inevitability or political desirability of the decline of the private landlord have blinded us to an aspect of the housing situation of our grandparents. When private renting was the norm, given the lower standards of services in housing that we take for granted today, there was considerable freedom of choice in the housing market, even for very poor families, and this resulted in a degree of dweller satisfaction which is much rarer when a multiplicity of landlords has given way to the monopoly of the local authority.

This was impressed on me by listening to hours of tape recordings of interviews with old people made by primary school children. Time and again the old ladies would say, 'Of course, you wouldn't understand, my dear, but in those days it was easy to move.' Their recollection is confirmed in a dozen working-class autobiographies. 'In the thirties,' recalls Elizabeth Ring, 'there was no such thing as a housing shortage. For from five shillings to five pounds a week, there were rooms for all.' Jack Common says of his childhood in Newcastle, 'At that time, families were always moving. There were houses to let everywhere.' Arthur Newton says of Hackney in East London, 'To change houses was easy then.' Mollie Weir from Glasgow describes with relish the many moves of her childhood and her mother's fondness for 'flitting', which in her family's context did not imply a 'moonlight flit'. 'How different everything looked,' she says, 'even if we'd only moved to the next close, which my mother did twice, for we knew our houses so intimately that the slightest variation in a lobby or a window-frame, or the size of a fireplace, was of enormous significance. Everybody loved a flitting. . . .'[7]

From a totally different background, the East End of London, A.S. Jasper in *A Hoxton Childhood*,[8] describes a whole series of childhood environments, starting in August 1910 when 'We were living at number three Clinger Street, Hoxton, in a hovel on the ground floor. It comprised two rooms with a kitchen, with an outside lavatory, which also served the family upstairs.' By page 15 we are told,

> It was agreed that Mother would try to find a bigger house. In those days it was easy; one had only to go to an agent, pay the first week's rent and move in. On more than one occasion my father came home late, drunk as usual, and was told by the next-door

neighbour we 'didn't live there any more'. We had owed so much rent but the fact was that we had to have a larger house. My mother duly found and inspected a house in Salisbury Street, New North Road. It wasn't a bad area and I always remember it was the nicest house we ever had.

And he describes with gusto how they set about redecorating it: 'Wallpaper was about threepence a roll; a ball of whitening and boiled size made whitewash for the ceilings.' But bad times came again, and on page 39 we hear, 'Our new abode was Ebenezer Buildings, Rotherfield Street. What a dump it was after the nice little house we had just left!' Soon his mother and sister went house hunting again and decided on a house in Loanda Street, by the side of the Regents Canal near the bridge in Kingsland Road. But a little later, 'Everything was getting too much for Mum and she reckoned the house had a curse on it. The only way was to move again. This time she found a house in Scawfell Street. This wasn't far from Loanda Street. It certainly looked a road with some life in it, which was what we were used to. Loanda Street was a drab place of flat-fronted houses where everyone closed their doors. There wasn't the friendliness.' But by page 88, 'We were now in 1917 and we were on the move again. Why, I cannot remember. This time we moved to Shepherdess Walk, off City Road. It was a very large house let off in flats. We had a ground floor and basement flat consisting of five large rooms and a scullery . . .' Not many pages later, in September 1918, 'We now lived in a very nice place in the main road. The rooms were large and there was always something going on.' But in the following year, the man who owned the dairy downstairs 'shocked us by saying that he was going to sell the dairy and we would have to quit the flat. He told us he had a house at Walthamstow we could rent and he would pay all the expenses if we would move. In 1919 Walthamstow to us was like moving to the country. The whole family discussed the matter and it was agreed they would go and see the place . . .' So, a couple of pages later in his narrative, they moved. 'It was a small house just off the High Street. The rent was eight shillings a week. I was beginning to like our new surroundings. For a penny you could get to Epping Forest, and this was all so different to the slums of Hoxton and Bethnal Green . . .'

Thus there were eight moves in Mr Jasper's childhood between the ages of four and fourteen. The moves were intimately related to shifts and changes in the family's minimal income and to the family size – whether his sister's husband was living with them or not, and so on. And the final move brought the family right out of the inner city and into the ampler opportunities of the leafy suburbs. With both Mr Jasper and Miss Weir, there glows through the pages what teachers are trained to call an 'affective relationship' between the family and its housing. This was the result of having, even among poor people, some degree of consumer choice. Changes in family circumstances as well as aesthetic preferences were reflected in the ability to move. Neither were they the families of skilled artisans. Miss Weir's father died when she was a baby and Mr Jasper's father was a drunken casual labourer. Both were effectively one-parent families.

Today, when the population of Glasgow and of Inner London are both dramatically lower than could have been imagined in those days, the element of freedom of choice and the opportunity for self-help in housing that those families had has totally disappeared.

When Peter Hall was given an opportunity to discuss the enormous and, to the public purse, expensive expansion of the architectural profession after the Second World War, he asked, 'Didn't it, unbelievably, result in an environment much worse than the one we had before?' And he went on to say,

> It's chastening to ask what would have happened if we'd never trained the architects, but had spent all that slum clearance money quite differently. Suppose, in the Liverpool of 1955, we hadn't said: 'a problem of replacing 88,000 unfit houses', but rather: 'a problem of making 88,000 houses fit', we could have given very generous improvement grants, encouraged small builders, opened DIY shops. The whole environment would have been improved piecemeal. It wouldn't have been very efficient – small-scale work never is – and besides, a good deal of the basic infrastructure would have had to be renewed. But it would have involved ordinary people in fixing up their own houses and helping improve their own neighbourhoods. It wouldn't have caused the enormous disruption, physical and social, that gave us the Everton Piggeries and the vandalized streets of Kirkby.[9]

By now most of us would agree with Peter Hall. I think myself that he understates the case. I am sure that piecemeal, dweller-controlled reconstruction would have been more efficient than anything that was actually inflicted on Liverpool, where enormous sums were paid out to the professionals, both inside the corporation and as outside consultants, from McKinseys and the most expensive urban planners down, for giving the worst possible advice. What did the ordinary tenant say, in a place like Cantrill Farm? – 'I wish I was back in the Dingle.' I think that Hall was wrong to single out the architects as responsible for the disasters of policy in Liverpool. The whole coalition of politicians, experts and administrators had a vested interest in not enabling people to find their own solutions. Ivan Illich remarks that

> In 1968, for example, it was still quite easy to dismiss organized lay resistance to professional dominance as nothing more than a throwback to romantic, obscurantist or elitist fantasies. The grass roots,

common-sense assessment of technological systems which I then outlined, seemed childish or retrograde to the political leaders of citizen activism, and to the 'radical' professionals who laid claim to the tutorship of the poor by means of their special knowledge. The reorganization of late industrial society around professionally defined needs, problems and solutions was still the commonly accepted value implicit in ideological, political, and juridical systems otherwise clearly and sometimes violently opposed to one another. Now the picture has changed . . .[10]

The picture has changed, even in Liverpool, as we shall see. But Liverpool was simply the most dramatic and poignant instance of the housing disasters of most British cities, including many London boroughs. This becomes clear whenever someone has taken the trouble to document the evolution and effect of housing policy in a particular place. One well-documented town in this respect is Sunderland, where Norman Dennis has described the workings of progressive housing policy in practice in two devastating books, *People and Planning* and *Public Participation and Planners Blight*. He shows with innumerable examples how, in the making of decisions affecting our environment, ordinary people's own perceptions of their housing and their own networks of self-help and mutual aid have been left entirely outside the calculation. (Where, in fact, in the days of vast public investment in housing, the life or death of a street could be made on a clip-board from the passenger seat of a moving council car.)

Norman Dennis talks about Millfield, a district of Sunderland, and the two ways of looking at the place. Within the first frame of reference, he says, 'Millfield, for example, is a collection of shabby, mean and dreary houses, derelict back lanes, shoddy-fronted shops and broken pavements, the whole unsightly mess mercifully ill-lit.'

A second frame of reference, that of, say, a 60-year-old woman living there, gives a very different picture:

> Millfield is Bob Smith's which she thinks (probably correctly) is the best butcher's in the town; George McKeith's wet-fish shop and Peary's fried-fish shop about which she says the same with equal justification; Maw's hot pies and peas, prepared on the premises; the Willow Pond public house, in which her favourite nephew organizes the darts and dominoes team; the Salvation Army band in a nearby street every Sunday and waking her with carols on Christmas morning; her special claim to attention at the grocers because her niece worked there for several years; the spacious cottage in which she was born and brought up, which she now owns, has improved, and which has not in her memory had defects which have caused either her or her neighbours discernible inconvenience (but which has some damp patches which make it classifiable as a 'slum dwelling'); the short road to the cemetery where she cares for the graves of her mother, father and brother; her sister's cottage across the road – she knows that every weekday at 12.30 a hot dinner will be ready for her when she comes from work; the bus route which will take her to the town centre in a few minutes; the homes of neighbours who since her childhood have helped her and whom she has helped; church, club and workplace within five minutes' walk; and, in general (as is said) 'every acre sweetened by the memory of the men who made us'.[11]

There is a terrible irony about the fact that public policy has frustrated both those people like A.S. Jasper's family who loved to be always on the move, and those, like the lady in Norman Dennis's account, who were ruthlessly uprooted from the social networks of self-help and mutual aid which sustained their lives, by the determination of local authorities to wipe out the past at the public expense. To me the description of Millfield evokes the way of life of many people I have known, as well as that of people I have casually interviewed in several British cities; others don't see it like that. Members of the audience at conferences about housing and planning to whom I've quoted this passage have seen it as just a sentimental evocation of the past.

The web of relationships, habits, associations and mutual obligations that formed the whole framework of that woman's life, was totally invisible to the politicians, the councillors, the Director of Housing, the Planning Officer and Director of Environment Services and the Medical Officer of Health. They reflected *her* history, not theirs. Professor A.H. Halsey has remarked on the radio that

> The movement which had invented the social forms of modern participatory democracy and practised it in union branch and co-op meeting was ironically fated to develop through its political party the bureaucratic corporate state ... And the supreme irony is that when a person like Norman Dennis protests against the emerging tyranny of government with the authentic voice of a deeply rooted English socialism, he is heard with approval by Sir Keith Joseph and dismissed as a nuisance by the Labour establishment.

People who insist on the importance of ordinary dwellers' perception, who declare that the important thing about housing is not what it *is* but what it *does* in the lives of its inhabitants, are often misrepresented as saying that people *like* having substandard housing, damp walls or an outside lavatory. They are, rather, saying that people's preferences, perceptions and choices are not only, perhaps not mainly, concerned with officially perceived housing standards, and that in any case, there is a gulf between these standards and what people want. In the first place, there is the indisputable truth that defects in your housing are infinitely more tolerable if they are *your* responsibility than if they are someone else's. In the second, there is the fact that housing policy has been, from its inception, intended to 'improve' or change people's domestic habits. And in the third, it has been based on the erroneous assumption that we are so short of land that people should be housed in flats.

Every study of ordinary people's wants, complaints and satisfactions, not just in Norman Dennis's studies in Sunderland, but those of others everywhere else, indicate that there is a certain kind of housing which over 80 per cent of English people prefer (I can't speak for the Welsh with their much higher proportion of owner-occupation or for the Scots with their lower one, much modified by the aspirations of the young). Their preference is for the ordinary small house with a back garden, traditionally provided, not just in the suburbs but in the cities themselves. But the public authorities, with their virtual monopoly of the provision of housing for rent, decided that an increasing proportion of people should be housed in a way which denied all their own desires.

Paralysed by a capitalist conception of land values, and aided by the lobby of the National Farmers' Union which urged that every last acre or hectare of unwanted wheat or barley would protect the country from urban infestation, it was felt that people should be protected from their own aspirations. And yet the housing that citizens actually yearn for is cheaper to build, infinitely cheaper to maintain and infinitely more adaptable to changing needs and demands.

Take one hilarious example: for generations, in municipal housing, the kitchen became smaller and smaller, in order to cure people of the reprehensible habit of eating in the kitchen. The result is that, up and down the land, you can meet families, squashed in a corner, taking turns at eating their meals on a table as big as a shelf. Meanwhile the socially conscious architect of the 'scheme' they have been obliged to inhabit, eats in his kitchen, surrounded by his family, off a scrubbed deal table, and his wife prides herself that their kitchen looks exactly like that of a Provençal peasant. There's a string of onions hanging from the beam of *her* kitchen ceiling in a house which is two miners' cottages joined together into one, in a Category D village to which Durham County Council has denied improvement grants.

The deliberate flouting of what people actually wanted didn't only happen in the North East. Ashley Bramall, a London Labour politician, remarks that the old County of London

> was mainly a city of small houses. Not only did the war scatter the population and destroy the homes, but it led to the rebuilding of London as a city of blocks of flats, of increasing height. This change has never been fully accepted by the population and there has been an increasing urge for movement to outer London and to the counties beyond, where the old pattern of street and house and garden could be recaptured.[12]

He blames the war for the habit of giving people the kind of housing they didn't want, just as Peter Hall blames the architects. Nowadays, in our present chastened mood, we say, 'But nobody told us at the time.' It isn't true. For it wasn't in 1975 or in 1965 or 1955 but in 1945 that Frederick Osborn, said, just as he had been saying at all those wartime conferences on postwar housing,

> I don't think philanthropic housing people anywhere realize the irresistible strength of the impulse towards the family house and garden as prosperity increases: they think that the suburban trend can be reversed by large-scale multi-storey buildings in the down-town districts, which is not merely a pernicious belief from a human point of view, but a delusion. In a few years' time the multi-storey technique will prove unpopular and will peter out. Damage will be done to society by

the trial, but probably all I can do is to hasten the
date of disillusion. If I have underestimated the
complacency of the urban masses, the damage may
amount to a disaster.[13]

What in fact he underestimated was the complacency of
the politicians and their professional advisers. In his book,
Towards a Humane Architecture, Bruce Allsop remarks, 'It is
astonishing with what savagery planners and architects are
trying to obliterate working-class cultural and social patterns.
Is it because many of them are first-generation middle-class
technosnobs?'[14]

Long familiarity with the housing problems industry tells
me he is right. If you are escaping from a history of poverty
and deprivation, you will simply see our old industrial areas
as a mean and cruel past, best expunged from the physical
environment as well as from the human memory. It is the
same with the councillors. If you have dedicated your lives
to the fight against capitalism and exploitation, you will, in
those areas of life like local government where you actually
win control, resolve to eliminate the mean streets, the shared
lavatories in the back yards and so on. And you will react
with outrage and a feeling of betrayal when people like
Norman Dennis conclude that *you*, the politician and the
professional, are the enemy, ruthlessly uprooting people
from familiar ways and familiar places. All those dedicated
chairs of housing and planning committees and their professional
employees weren't consciously conducting a battle
against the weak and poor. They had simply absorbed the
message of their times: firstly, that the only possible approach
to housing was wholesale clearance and redevelopment in
vast building contracts, and secondly, that people's own
capacity for self-help and mutual aid was totally irrelevant
to their housing.

3. Is selling off a sell-out?

Most capitalist working classes now include two or three distinct 'tenure classes – households who own their housing, those who rent it from private landlords, and in some countries a third class who rent it from public landlords. The same wages structures hold for them all regardless of their housing tenures, and in defiance of Engels' expectations, the housing tenures make large differences to the people's fortunes. Over their household lifetimes the home owners commonly average between a quarter and a half better off than the tenants of private landlords, in what they have to spend or save after taxes and housing costs. They often also have better housing and domestic productivity. Most of the difference consists of income which tenants transfer to landlords, and home owners do not. It can add up to many years' income over a household's lifetime. Scarcely any of the differences between owners' and tenants' fortunes are cancelled by wage movements as Engels expected them to be. So it seems sensible (and also Marxist!) to see housing and domestic equipment as capital means of production. Landlords who own those means of production can appropriate surplus value from tenants; households which own their own capital escape that exploitation.
    Hugh Stretton, *Urban Planning in Rich and Poor Countries*, 1978.

In the summer of 1983, in the wake of the most serious electoral defeat of the political Left for generations, I was invited to attend the conference at Nottingham University of Shelter, the National Campaign for the Homeless. The opening address was given by Cllr David Blunkett, leader of Sheffield City Council, and it was rapturously received. I sat in the front row and took careful note of his remarks.

He attacked the Conservative government's policy which had virtually ended the building of new houses by local authorities, he attacked its 'right to buy' legislation and explained that his council was doing its utmost within the law to delay and circumvent its application. He ridiculed the aspiration to own one's own home as socially divisive individualism, but at the same time explained his fellow councillors' difficulties in attempting to devise more responsive forms of housing management.

In one of his many entertaining asides he explained that the moment the word decentralization was mentioned, the housing staff shuffled the papers around to calculate how many stages up the salary scale they would climb if local management was instituted. And he went on to talk about 'the iron grip that many councils have on the throat of their tenants' and about the way that, as he put it, 'welfarism has degenerated into paternalism'. 'By God,' he said, 'it's a terrible bureaucracy we're fighting against.'

He was followed by Ed Berman, the abrasive director of the charity Interaction. Berman's technique, at this meeting of a crusade for the homeless, which was in fact a get-together of the professionals of the housing problems industry, was to ask which members of his audience were council tenants and which were owner-occupiers. Needless to say, the former category was very small, while the overwhelming majority at the gathering included Mr Blunkett, Mr Berman, the Director of Shelter and me. Mr Berman asked how it was possible to have a centralized housing policy without a governmental and municipal bureaucracy with its own vested interests. 'If you cut off its head,' he declared, 'it will grow back tenfold.'

This was a promising start, I thought, for an honest discussion of the double standard we apply to housing: our own and other people's. But the issue that dominated that conference was 'the right to buy' and not at all that of homelessness. We had to wait for the last of the invited speakers, Malcolm Wicks, to urge that there was nothing necessarily socialist about council housing nor anything necessarily capitalist about owner-occupation. ('Just as well,' commented another housing pundit, Bernard Kilroy, telling us that 54 per cent of skilled manual workers own their own homes.) But Mr Wicks also made a comment which, although it is part of every family's everyday experience, seldom reaches the people who earn a living as authorities on housing.

He suggested that our housing needs vary at different stages of the family life cycle. The footloose young, away from the family nest, assuming that they had one, just need a pad, cheap to rent by the week, instantly available and instantly quittable. Isn't it incredible that in a rich and sophisticated society it is hard to find this simple basic need? The couple, when they rear a family, equally obviously need a house with a garden, capable of being adapted to the enormous variety of family needs, both economic and recreational, that arise today. By common consent from an overwhelming majority of people, including those in places where flat-dwelling is traditional, this need is best met by the owner-occupied house. Other forms of housing and of tenure are regarded as a substitute for this ideal. But a huge number of households actually consist of single people or pairs, or of people whose children have left home but who delight in the space to welcome their children and grandchildren, or who are old and just want a cheap and troublefree roof over their heads. Their demands on the housing system range from a place with absolute security and no worries at all about maintenance, to a place where they can make themselves a fulltime occupation in the task of caring for, cherishing and improving, not just their own place but those of everyone else around. Who cuts the grass and nurtures the daffodils?

I may have put words into his mouth, but for me the bright spot of that conference (just as in Shelter's 1984 conference the bright spot was Ken Atkins talking about the way self-build had totally changed the lives of the builders) was the recognition that people have changing demands on the housing system at different stages in life, and that any society, whether we call it primitive, traditional, capitalist or socialist, has to find some way of meeting these changing needs. They are all so simple and sensible that it seems absurd that in a mixed economy society we can't manage to meet them for a sizeable section of our fellow citizens. The same difficulty afflicted Vladimir Voinovich, a manual worker from Soviet Central Asia, who, in a country which for 68 years had attempted to remove housing from the market economy, just wanted a room of his own.

In *The Ivankiad: Or the Tale of the Writer Voinovich's Installation in His New Apartment*[1] he describes in the most excruciating and tedious detail his struggles with the socialized housing system. This book made me reflect again on Tony Judge's comment on 'the insufferably paternalistic attitudes of councils and officials to their tenants', and on David Blunkett's remark that 'it's a terrible bureaucracy we're fighting against.'

This is why it was possible for Michael Heseltine, Conservative Secretary of State for the Environment, to say in introducing the statutory right to buy in the 1980 Housing Act, that it would 'transform the personal prospects of millions of individuals above the bureaucracies of the state.' What we on the Left find hard to swallow is the large element of truth in all that hyperbole. Personally I am hostile to the implications of the 1980 Housing Act because I see it as one more nail in the coffin of local decision making. I want decisions, right or wrong, Right or Left, to be made locally. But the opposition to the right to buy legislation hasn't been on these grounds.

The sale of council houses to sitting tenants is no new thing. It wasn't invented by the dreadful Thatcher-Heseltines. According to David Donnison, 'a total of 95,900 council houses were sold between 1974 and 1979, for most of which time Labour was in power at Westminster.'[2] Visiting estates on the outskirts of London, Cardiff and Birmingham even earlier, I used to fear the socially divisive effect of individual sales, and was intrigued to find that in fact they had pushed up the standard of environmental maintenance all round. And when you look at those dreary estates, what a change that made!

The notion that sales to tenants diminishes the nation's stock of houses is demonstrably false. Citizens are housed, whether they are paying rent or mortgage repayments, and if they decide to sell their houses, somebody will still get housed. The argument that council house sales reduce the pool of housing at the council's disposal is only half true because of the awful inflexibility of letting policy. Houses likely to be sold are never likely to join the pool because the tenant taking advantage of the offer is seldom a candidate in the open market. If they don't buy they will remain a tenant of the same house, and so will the surviving spouse or resident children on the tenant's death. (Unlike some commentators, I regard this 'inheritance' of a tenancy as a desirable thing which would be taken for granted in other sectors of the housing market.)

I would argue in fact that the transfer of council houses to their occupants is the best guarantee of their survival. Everyone knows of the sad decline into obsolescence of the interwar and early postwar estates. Councils blame the cuts. More thoughtful people reflect that local authority housing is the only sector in which houses have a limited life. Owner-occupied housing goes on for ever. It is improved, extended and updated, by one generation after another. No-one would dream of suggesting that its useful life was over. Even when the old lady who has lived in a house for generations has been unable to spend money on repairs and renovations, some incoming couple will rejoice that its disrepair is reflected in the price, and they set about the adventure of reconstruction to their own desires. Often they are pleased that no-one has replaced the old panelled doors with their modern hardboard flush equivalent, or removed the Victorian fireplaces or Edwardian ironmongery.

In the council sector everything is different. For many years many councils would threaten tenants with eviction if they dared to replace the pea-green distemper with their own wallpaper. Nowadays the enormous cost of employing anyone to do anything has ensured that most councils are only too pleased if a tenant redecorates or repairs. In fact in their characteristically authoritarian way, some are unilaterally rewriting tenancy agreements to make tenants responsible for repairs without any recognition that this transfer of responsibility should be rewarded. When the council does get around to modernizing the estate, it does so in one vast expensive operation which often does not meet tenants' own perception of their needs. In one city I visited, my host took me to see the dump where improving owner-occupiers were looting the vitreous-enamelled cast iron baths which the council was taking out of the whole estate, to replace them with the up-to-date flimsy fibreglass kind.

Of course the occupiers are the people who should be in control of repairs and renovations. The alternative is either grotesquely expensive outside contracts or a direct labour organization with, as David Blunkett put it in his engagingly honest remarks at Nottingham, 'workers and tenants hating each other'. Dweller control of housing, whether individual or collective, ensures that the enormous public investment in housing in the past is rescued rather than wasted. The tenant's right to buy does pose one genuine problem for councils. In their housing revenue accounts councils operate a pooling arrangement of rents and subsidies so that their older properties, let at figures way above the economic rent or historic cost, subsidize the newer ones built at astronomical cost in the 1970s. In other words, the tenants of old council property, who may well have lived there for decades, are subject to continually rising rents to help keep down the rents of new council property. Under no conceivable ethical system can it be considered just that the poor should be obliged to subsidize the poor under compulsion, when the rich feel no such obligation.

There is a grotesque disparity between the two main sectors of the housing market. I am not referring to tax relief on mortgage interest which socialists regard as a subsidy to the owner-occupier – no elected government of the Left will remove this advantage since governments depend on the marginal votes in marginal parliamentary constituencies in the owner-occupation belt. I am simply talking about the fact that to owner-occupiers, the cost of housing while it may be high at the beginning, tends, thanks to continuing inflation, to decline as time goes by. However large a proportion of income goes on mortgage repayments in the early years, it gets smaller all through the life of the mortgage and becomes trivial when the mortgagee pays off the last instalments and lives happily ever after. Council tenants are in a quite different situation. Whatever the council's policy and whatever its political complexion, rents rise continually over the years, in ways which bear no relation to the paying off of the original cost of the building. At the end of their working lives, as they join the inevitable queue for housing benefit, they have nothing at all to show for their lifetime investment in their own homes, except a full rent book.

I imagine that readers, even socialist readers, have little idea of how council rent policy victimizes tenants, and they probably haven't quite woken up to the fact that tenants are by now actually in the position of subsidizing owner-occupiers' rates. Most of our assumptions about council tenancy are still based on the idea that the private householder was subsidizing the council tenant. (Hence all the querulous comments we used to hear from the commuters about the Jags parked on the council estate.) Let me quote from Macey and Baker, the textbook used by students on housing management:

> For many years after 1945 many local authorities were still charging prewar rents at absurdly low levels having regard to the real value of the commodity offered. There was resistance among tenants to the placing of a proper value on the houses and an unwillingness to regard them as assets belonging to the community. There was also a tendency to plead that the tenants of prewar houses had paid for them twice over. Such statements were often based on the rent including rates, and no allowance was made for the changing costs of management and maintenance. In fact, although most prewar houses are now let at more realistic rents, showing a surplus, it will in most cases be many years before this surplus wipes out the cumulative loss over the first 25 or so years in the life of a dwelling.[3]

The authors provide the following calculation: assume a house built in 1930 with a cost rent of 67p weekly. (Cost rent is the rent at which a house must be let in order to cover loan interest and sinking fund contribution, and the cost of maintenance and management.) Deduct from this the exchequer subsidy of 15p and the (then) statutory rate fund contribution of 8p, leaving a subsidized rent of 44p as the actual rent in 1930. They then examine the position in 1964, with a cost rent of 102p (increased to cover the 1964 cost of repairs, management and incidentals). Deduct from this the exchequer subsidy of 15p, and you get a subsidized rent of 87p. But, they say, the actual net rent since 1963 has been 135p, leaving a weekly contribution of 48p to the rents pool. And they go on to say that, 'By 1971 the position might well have been that the historic cost rent had risen to £1.50 per week compared with a fair rent of, say £3.50 per week.'

But using their figures, and assuming the 'worst' case, i.e. that the rent only went up from 44p to 135p in 1963, and from that to £3.50 in 1971, the cumulative loss would have been wiped out by 1973! Assuming the initial cost of the house to have been £350, the cost rent would have paid for the house in 10 years, while in the tenants' view the actual rent would have paid for the house in 15 years, so it is easy to see why they considered they had paid for it twice over by 1960, and why by 1971 they could not conceive that it was just to be paying £1.50 in historic cost rent and another £2.00 into the rent pool.

These arcane calculations may seem absurd nowadays, but in 1974 I published a further calculation based on them to follow the family fortunes of the tenants of such a house.[4] Imagine yourself as an actual tenant who moved into the estate when the house was new and who is now retired. Had you been a little better paid or in more regular employment at the time, you could have clambered onto the interwar owner-occupation bandwaggon. 'The New Ideal Homesteads £295 house was obtainable in 1932–3 for 9s a week plus rates, while the repayments for the Hilbery Chaplin £345 house were only 8s 5d.'[5] The mortgage would have been paid off years ago and the 'current market value' of the house – probably not as well built originally as the council house you actually got – would be by 1985, judging by advertisements in estate agents windows, up to £40,000. But suppose that you have died by now and your son or daughter has 'inherited' your tenancy (in the way that used to bring such sneers about the 'featherbedding' of council tenants). Would *you* feel responsible for 'the cumulative loss over the first 25 or so years in the life of a dwelling' or for paying far more into the rent pool than as historic rent?

What you would know is that the son or daughter of the other fellow (who in 1930 was earning £3 a week in a steady job instead of the £2.75 you earned in an insecure one) has, for a far smaller total outlay by his or her late father, inherited thousands of pounds worth of house with no obligation to regard it as an asset belonging to the council rather than to its users. (This may be an argument against the principle of inheritance, but *that* is on no-one's agenda!)

The council tenants' situation, which was always less advantageous by comparison with that of the owner-occupier, has dramatically worsened in recent years. They are by now the helpless victims of the whims of central government. Far from being subsidized by other ratepayers or by central grants, their typical situation was calculated by Stephen Hilditch of Shelter in September 1983 as being one in which 'the majority of councils are now making profits on their council houses'. Not only this, their rents are determined entirely by the government's annual budgetary strategy. Hence the Chancellor's announcement on 11 November 1983 that rents must go up by an average of 75p a week. A study published by the Policy Studies Institute shows that council tenants' rents rose by 113 per cent between 1979 and 1984.[6]

During the Wilson and Callaghan governments, Peter Walker, the former Conservative Secretary of State for the Environment, went round the country making speeches in which he proposed his own version of the tenants' charter which he, rightly, described as a great deal more genuine than the phoney consultation exercises about the colour of front doors which other people described by that name. He was suggesting that local authorities should transform long-term council tenants into owner-occupiers by *giving* them their homes. When he replied to his critics that this would be the most effective and immediate way of achieving a radical redistribution of property in this country, he was calling the bluff of the sanctimonious hypocrisy that surrounds the politics of housing in Britain. His view was shared, in those days, by Frank Field, then director of the Child Poverty Action Group and subsequently Labour MP for Birkenhead.[7] I agreed with them, for by the late 1970s we were beginning to experience the farcical situation where, in several London boroughs, the cost of management and maintenance exceeded the rent income. This is no longer true, partly because of the enormous rent rises since then and partly because councils have a new scapegoat for their neglect of maintenance in the Conservative government's cuts in public expenditure. What reader acquainted with the facts of housing finance would not advise any tenant who is able to get out from under this arbitrary treatment to do so if they can? And if this is the advice we would all give privately, why don't we say the same thing publicly? We could then, instead of conducting a phoney crusade against the right to buy, concentrate on getting the principles of housing right and on avoiding the dreadful mistakes made in the era of authoritarian paternalism.

4. Learning from the poor

Particularly in house construction and land development the *barriada* people have done better than the government, and at much less cost. The failures of governments and private developers everywhere to provide low-cost housing for the poor are notorious. Administrative costs, bureaucratic restrictions and the high cost of materials and construction when government agencies do the contracting generally put the housing rentals beyond the reach of the lowest-income group. Equally disappointing are the failures in the design of this official public housing, which usually disregards the desires and style of life of the people for whom it is intended.

In the Peruvian *barriadas*, by avoiding government control and the requirements of lending institutions, the people have built houses to their own desires and on the basis of first things first. Because they needed shelter immediately, they built walls and a roof and left bathrooms and electricity to be added later. They want flat roofs and strong foundations so that they can add a second storey. They want a yard for raising chikens and guinea pigs, and a front room that can serve as a store or a bar-room. They have dispensed with the restrictive residential zoning and construction details that middle-class planners and architects consider essential for proper housing.

William Mangin, 'Squatter settlements', *Scientific American*, October 1967.

Everyone today laments the way Britain's great cities are falling apart and attributes their plight and their problems to the collapse of the industries which gave rise to their mushroom growth in the nineteenth century. We tend to forget that when Birmingham, Manchester, Newcastle, Liverpool or Glasgow were in their heyday, when the docks were full of ships and the heavy industries loaded with orders, these cities were bywords for deprivation and squalor. Their overcrowding, their epidemics and their incredible mortality rates were at their worst when the city's economy was booming.

The drama of instant urban growth is being played out today in the cities of the Third World – of Latin America, Africa and Asia – where in the last 40 years urban populations have grown in a way that has been even more awesome than that of the industrial cities of Britain and America in the last century. There is a crucial difference of course. In our cities industrialization preceeded urban growth and rural immigrants came to town to meet the demand for factory labour, urged on by enclosures and changes in farming methods that made the lives of country workers even more poverty-stricken than before. But in the Third World urbanization has preceeded industrialization: people have moved to the cities in vast numbers before there has been any likelihood of their finding work in the regular employment market.

They have done so because they have calculated that the chances for their children, if not for themselves, in basic medical care, education and in eventual work prospects, will be better in the city than in the stagnant rural economy. However much it may suit their country's rulers to have the peasantry quietly starving in the backlands, this has usually been a rational decision: the enormous gamble and family upheaval involved in moving out of the traditional rural background, *have* proved to be worth enduring, for millions. The anthropologist Lisa Peattie told me of her puzzlement when she first went to Bogotà. There seemed to be no economic base to sustain the exploding population, but no-one looked ill-nourished and everyone was shod. She realized eventually that beside the official economy that figured in the statistics, there was an unofficial, invisible, informal economy of tiny enterprises and service occupations which provided purchasing power for the unofficial population. Obviously there must be a point where diminishing returns begin to be observable. A salutory study of the refuse recyclers of Cali, Colombia, concludes, 'The garbage picker may work hard, may have a shrewd eye for saleable materials, may search long for the right buyer; in short, he may be the near-perfect example of the enterprising individual. It will not get him far.'[1]

But still the cities of the Third World grow. There is an observable pattern of movement. People come to the same inner city area as their relations or compatriots from the same village or province. They pay an exorbitant rent for a share of the grossly overcrowded city slums. After they have become used to urban ways, which often involves adaptation to a different language and culture, they conclude that their present needs and future prospects would be better met in one of the sprawling new unofficial settlements that ring every capital city in the Third World. These shanty towns and squatter townships have a variety of names in different countries: *barrios*, *barriadas*, *favelas*, *ranchos*, *gourbivilles*, *gececondu*, *bustees* or *colonias miserias*, and for decades have been regarded with horror by the rich, the governing elite and by the visiting Westerners, speeding past from the airport to the Hilton Hotel.

In many countries, notoriously South Africa, but also under a dozen allegedly more liberal regimes, extreme measures were and are taken to eliminate them, with the police and the army burning down the straw huts or uprooting the corrugated iron shanties, and 'resettling' the inhabitants in some remote place where there was not the slightest chance of their gaining a livelihood. (It happened in our own history in the Highland clearances.) In others, grandiose schemes for rehousing the unofficial citizens have been embarked upon. The most famous was probably that of the 'superblocks' of the 1950s into which the national guard of the Venezuelan dictator Perez Jimenez decanted the squatters:

> By the time the dictatorship finally collapsed the superblocks were in social chaos which, even now, has only been partially resolved. The incomplete and unoccupied apartments and many community buildings were invaded, controlled by gangs, the utilities and even the lifts broke down, the facilities were totally inadequate, the groups were often isolated by difficult communications from the rest of the city, and, on top of these and many other difficulties, the political situation made it extremely difficult to do anything at all.[2]

We have no reason at all to smile at the absurdities involved in Latin-American housing policies. Haven't we all watched with glee the film of the blowing up of the prize-winning Pruitt-Igoe housing at St Louis, or of housing at Birkenhead and Leeds for similar reasons?

Slowly voices began to be heard which reflected not the official outside perception of a 'problem', but the inside view of the dweller, just as Norman Dennis, cited in Chapter 2, took the revolutionary step of looking at Sunderland's 'slum' housing from the standpoint of the people who inhabit it. Take the squatter settlements on the fringe of Rio de Janeiro, as seen by the visiting philanthropist:

> From outside, the typical *favella* seems a filthy, congested human antheap. Women walk back and forth with huge metal cans of water on their heads or cluster at the communal water supply washing clothes. Men hang around the local bars chatting or playing

cards, seemingly with nothing better to do. Naked children play in the dirt and mud. The houses look precarious at best, thrown together out of discarded scraps. Open sewers create a terrible stench, especially on hot, still days. Dust and dirt fly everywhere on windy days, and mud cascades down past the huts on rainy ones.[3]

Janice Perlman, in her study of *The Myth of Marginality*, urges us to see beyond the visual squalor, and grasp, just for once, the way the inhabitants feel about it:

Things look very different from inside, however. Houses are built with a keen eye to comfort and efficiency, given the climate and available materials. Much care is evident in the arrangement of furniture and the neat cleanliness of each room. Houses often boast colourfully painted doors and shutters, and flowers or plants on the window sill. Cherished objects are displayed with love and pride. Most men and women rise early and work hard all day. Often these women seen doing laundry are earning their living that way, and many of the men in bars are waiting for the work shift to begin. Children, although often not in school, appear on the whole to be bright, alert and generally healthy. Their parents . . . place high value on giving them as much education as possible. Also unapparent to the casual observer, there is a remarkable degree of social cohesion and mutual trust and a complex internal social organization, involving numerous clubs and voluntary associations.[4]

The change in our perception of 'the cities the poor build' in the Third World has been largely due to the work of an English architect, John Turner, and an American anthropologist, William Mangin, whose experience in the shanty towns of Lima in the 1950s and 1960s has since been paralleled by that of many other observers all over the world. Andrew Hake, for example, worked in Nairobi, which he found to be a two-faced city, with a modern face to the outside world but a growing number of people in the backyard. These backyard inhabitants, to whom the reactions of the city authorities have ranged from uncomprehending hostility to total demolition without resettlement, are in his view, 'an immense potential for creative development which will determine the future shape of the city, and contribute enormously to the country's well-being'. By 1971, a third of Nairobi's population were living in unauthorized housing:

> They had probably created by that time something over 50,000 jobs which did not appear in any official statistics. They had built many elements of an urban infrastructure and had created patterns of social organization to maintain the fabric of the self-help society, with a variety of cultures including adaptations of Kikuyu life on the rural ridges, the Islamic tradition of the older coastal Swahili men in Pumwani and of the Sudanese veterans in Kibera, the beer-brewing women and the flashy, self-conscious modernization of the teenagers. The self-help city is now building more houses, creating more jobs, absorbing more people, and growing faster, than the modern city.[5]

And not only this. It is also less vulnerable to the fluctuations of the official capitalist economy, and 'it can absorb the casualties of the modern development process.' The self-help city, he claims, provides income and a measure of status for 'hundreds of thousands who would otherwise be in even greater deprivation in overpopulated rural areas'. Andrew Hake does not believe that self-help is a substitute for social justice. He thinks that in the coming decades there will be increasing awareness that the modern city 'will be dependent upon and living off the backs of the self-help city and the informal sector'; and he asks how much conspicuous consumption and luxury living the future city will tolerate.

Turner's experience in Peru, stressing that self-help housing housed far more people, more effectively, than any government programme, stressed that, given favourable circumstances, the settlement of straw huts evolved over time into fully serviced, permanently constructed suburbs. It led to his paper at the 1966 United Nations seminar on Uncontrolled Urban Settlements, which was most influential in persuading international funding bodies and government agencies to set in motion 'site-and-services' housing programmes, about which he himself has reservations:

> Not unreasonably or unnaturally official policies began to call for 'harnessing' and 'mobilizing' these popular forces and resources – especially those supported by international agencies whose personnel generally have far more liberal views than found in the governments they advised, whatever their hidden roles may be in the international system. The implications of words like 'harnessing' and 'mobilizing' tend to reinforce an elitist assumption that underlies and even motivates certain self-help lobbies. The elitist assumption is that *the* resources of 'the people' or 'the masses' are in their hands and the strength of their bodies. Their heads, by implication, are rather small. Intelligence, it is commonly assumed, is a function of schooling and this is a commodity controlled by the elites which are composed of those who have access to 'higher education' – that is, anything beyond basic reading, writing and arithmetical skills that citizens must have in order to read and carry out instructions. So the reformed image of government housing action and urban development can be caricatured as that of a small minority of swollen-headed but manually incompetent officers ordering about an army of the strong-armed but pin-headed masses.[6]

From his experience in Latin America Turner moved to the United States and in the end back to Britain. He found that the principles he had deduced in the poor world were equally true of the richest countries in the world. His general conclusion about housing is expressed in the following proposition:

> When dwellers control the major decisions and are free to make their own contribution to the design, construction or management of their housing, both the process and the environment produced stimulate individual and social well-being. When people have no control over, nor responsibility for key decisions in the housing process, on the other hand, dwelling environments may instead become a barrier to personal fulfilment and a burden on the economy.[7]

This is a carefully worded statement that says no more and no less than it means. Notice that he says 'design, construction *or* management.' He is not implying, as critics sometimes suggest, that the poor of the world should become do-it-yourself housebuilders, though of course in practice they very often have to be. He is simply saying that they should be in control of the process. Turner believes that 'while local control over necessarily diverse personal and local goods and services – such as housing – is essential, local control depends on personal and local access to resources which only central government can guarantee.' At the same time he is sceptical, as a result of his own early experience in Arequipa, Peru, about government-controlled self-help:

> We spent enormous amounts of time and energy – working seven evenings a week for over a year on top of normal office hours – to organize people into groups quite unnecessarily, to buy and distribute materials they could get more cheaply themselves, and trying to get them to do building work by complicated

rotas when they preferred to hire their own labourers. We quite failed to appreciate the nature and economy of direct action that people had been taking all along and with enormous and unnecessary effort introduced a far less efficient system which failed to make proper use of the resources with which the immense number of houses all around our own project dwellings were being built. As I eventually learned, the economy of their own forms of self-help was based on the capacity and freedom of individuals and small groups to make their own decisions, *more* than on their own capacity to do manual work.[8]

The heroic saga of the cities poor people build for themselves has been going on long enough by now to have become *the* great and relatively peaceful success story of the twentieth century. It hasn't made news precisely because we would rather sit at home sympathizing with the Third World poor, or wishing on them whichever variety of revolution we haven't actually achieved at home. The politicians at a local level, whether of Left, Right or centre, have almost all been obliged to woo the unofficial citizens rather than to eliminate them. From being a force to be ignored, uprooted or continually browbeaten, they have become a franchise to be cultivated.

At a bureaucratic and technocratic level, both nationally and internationally, these citizens are still regarded with suspicion, and the very firms of multinational consultants who once regarded them as a squalid nuisance, now want to incorporate their energy in the rationalization of any Third World city you care to think about. The people whose mode of thinking built the new capital city of Brasilia don't relish the fact that the only economically healthy aspect of its economy is in the ring of self-built unofficial satellite towns – Cidade Livre, Taguatinga, Sobiadinho and Gama – which were rushed up for themselves by the workers drawn into the area to build the new city of the bureaucrats.

Nor do the world-famous designers of Chandigarh, capital of Punjab, and the city administrators, like to be reminded of the way they totally ignored the vital importance of the 'non-plan' market traders in their city's economy. In 'direct contradiction to the state's own open commitment to removing poverty and reducing inequality', the authorities in that city applied a policy of 'constant persecution, humiliation and harassment' to the petty traders, and finally, in the face of ordinary realities, known to every poor person from Moscow to Manilla, introduced policies from which 'it was principally the richer ones who benefited.'[9]

There is, needless to say, a Marxist critique of the self-help ideology of housing. Hans Harms, who provides a most interesting account of historic examples, notes that 'Self-help housing as a policy solution to housing problems in capitalist societies has occurred with great regularity throughout history, invariably when there is a crisis in capitalism.' In his view,

1. Self-help housing provides possibilities (a) to lower the level of circulation of capital in housing; (b) to increase the amount of unpaid labour in society; (c) to devalorize labour power and to lower pressure for wage increases by excluding housing costs from wages.
2. It reduces the need for public subsidies to housing, since the reproduction of labour is done by the efforts and costs of labour itself.
3. It is economically expansionary for consumption demands.
4. Ideologically it incorporates people into the mentality of the petty bourgeoisie to own and speculate with housing.
5. It isolates people from each other; it can individualize discontent and preempts collective actions and solidarity.[10]

Similarly, the geographer, Rod Burgess, claims that the squatter is simply in the 'petty-commodity' business: 'He has not escaped capitalism – he is merely in another part of it.' For him, 'Squatter settlements allow a large, permanent industrial reserve army of labour to be cheaply installed in the cities. They also minimize housing and land costs and extend family budgets through landlordism and horticulture. The reduction of food and housing costs reduces pressure for wage increases.'[11]

Alas, these comments illustrate what a grotesque distorting mirror Marxist economic analysis applies to reality. Squatter settlers on the fringes of the cities of the poor countries would wonder how their vegetable-growing could reduce their non-existent wages and would certainly ask for the address of the recruiting offices of that famous reserve army of labour.

Nor would the interpretation of self-help housing by Western academic Marxists make sense to the citizens of those countries where the official theology is Marxism. In Cuba, for example, Fidel Castro has admitted that concentration on other social and economic goals has led to housing being given a disastrously low priority in the city of Havana. But at the same time, in the new residential settlements on the fringe and in the country there is an absolute reliance on a state-controlled version of the self-help solution, where prospective occupants of multistorey flats, designed for erection by non-professional labour, are organized into 'micro-brigades' to do the building in their free time, though the completed building is to be owned not by the occupant-builders but by the state. In the Chinese city of Shanghai, when a neighbourhood committee decided to build three blocks of flats, they were erected by the self-help labour of the people of the neighbourhood, supervised by two skilled builders. More recently, 'City dwellers in China will be encouraged to buy their own houses or flats as part of a new scheme to deal with serious housing shortages. The state will also help people to build their own homes and provide them with the materials.'¹² In the country, when a couple marry, the commune provides a site and materials and the family and neighbours build the house by voluntary labour.

But it is in the matured and dynastic Marxist states of Eastern Europe that the self-help ideology of the citizens has been best integrated into the way in which the official housing system works. The high level of home ownership there ('incorporating people into the mentality of the petty bourgeoisie') especially among the Marxist intelligentisia, reflects the fact that ordinary pragmatism implies that the owner-occupied dwelling, like the peasant's private plot (where horticulture both 'extends family budgets' and ensures that citizens can actually buy fruit and vegetables), is regarded as personal property like clothing or furniture, rather than as real property like the landlord's estate.

The planning policy of 'containing' the cities has resulted in large numbers of urban dwellers regarding their state flat as a weekday pied-à-terre, while their real family home and eventual retirement home is in the self-built 'wild settlements', seen by Western bankers as they travel by official limousine from the airport to the city centre, at say Nowy Dwór outside Warsaw, or Kozarski Bok outside Zagreb, or on the slopes of Mount Vitosha outside Sofia. Every fifth household in Prague has one of these homes in the hinterland, and it is not really surprising that people devote their loving spare-time care to improving, decorating and enlarging them, rather than to cherishing their inner-city pad.[13]

Contrary to capitalist rumours, although the upper classes of the Soviet Union have their dashas in exclusive zones like Serebryanny Bor, other people have struggled to make a place in the sun. Dennis Shaw cites an article by the Soviet writer, V. Kherkel, who under the title *Vasha Dasha* (meaning '*Your* Dasha' and implying his readers' everyday familiarity with the idea) observes that gardening has often become only secondary to general leisure on the co-operatives in Estonia; while outside Moscow 'some summer garden chalets constructed in the 1950s already have central heating and an obvious air of permanency'; and though around Leningrad 'many dashas are uncomfortable, poorly constructed and situated either in areas which are aesthetically poor or on land that would be better put to other purposes', they 'continue to play an extremely important role in the hinterland of the larger city, catering for 93 per cent of rest places around the city of Leningrad and 62 per cent around Moscow'.[14]

In Romania, in an edict that achieved at one stroke the ultimate aim of the Thatcher government in Britain, the government obliged tenants to buy their state flats or houses individually, or to face rent increases of up to 100 per cent.[15] I asked a Yugoslav economist why house purchase was so actively encouraged in his country and he replied that personal investment in the dwelling was thought desirable since it both reduced the disposable income available for the purchase of scarce consumer goods and reduced the enormous charge on the state's budget for housing provision.

In Hungary, the country whose second-highest export is humorists, the local wits point out that 'it took a communist revolution to give Hungarian cities an exclusively middle-class character'[16] because all the really good urban housing is by now monopolized by the ruling and managerial elites, usually at subsidized rents, while most unskilled industrial workers commute from private housing in the hinterland.[17] But the best of all eulogies for the self-help sector in housing comes from a dissident Hungarian writer, Janos Kenedi in his book *Do it Yourself*,[18] where he describes in hilarious detail how he built his own house in the informal economy. He claims that since the government has taken on itself the awe-inspiring task of housing the entire population, he, in shouldering the burden of providing his own house, was patriotically enabling the state to concentrate on more deserving cases.

The best and saddest epitaph for the Marxist approach to housing was written by an Australian economist, Hugh Stretton, who observed:

> Pathetically, Russian town dwellers go out and comb the countryside for patches of neglected land they can plant, visit, enjoy, 'make their own' however tenuously. Their masters, who own everything just as the masters did in Marx's day, discourage this petit-bourgeois practice. In that and other ways they do their best to build for twenty-first-century Russia the urban fabric of nineteenth-century Manchester. Plenty of left as well as right technocrats are doing the same for the working-class quarters of west European cities. The hard Left – Marxist and technocratic – thus works as hard as any capitalist to kill the most promising of all socialist opportunities, and to perpetuate the alienation which Marx condemned as the worst effect of primitive industrial capitalism.[19]

There is a well-known saying of Tolstoy's about the way the rich man will do anything for the poor man except get off his back. In housing, it turns out to be true of every country in the world. Given half a chance people will house themselves and for the greater part of human history in the greater part of the world they have done so. Asked what housing lesson we can learn from the poor, John Turner suggests that we borrow a well-known rhetorical style and conclude that never before did so many do so much with so little. And he suggests that when we contemplate the projects intended to house or rehouse the masses through corporate agencies, public or private, capitalist or communist, our only possible conclusion is that never before was so little done for so many with so much.

5. Plots of freedom

> The house took me and the wife 11 months to build. It was a very enjoyable experience after the time involved in getting the scheme off the ground. It is an adaptable building, unusual yes, but extremely nice to live in. The sheer joy of putting a spade in the ground . . . well it's an indescribable feeling . . . you finally have control over what you are doing in your life.
>
> Ken Atkins of Lewisham Self-Build Housing Association, 1983

In our album there's a photograph of a house. I don't know if it's my mother or my aunt standing outside the bay window. But I can tell from her clothes that the snapshot was taken in about 1913 when the house was new. I can tell too, from the fact that the new house is behind an old hedge, with a bridge built over the ditch, that the house belongs to that period of agricultural depression when plots of land on the fringe of the city were literally dirt cheap.

It was built for his own family by my grandfather, who was a carpenter, but who could evidently turn his hand to bricklaying and the other building skills. It is typical of (or, I might argue, slightly superior to) the millions of suburban houses built all over this country in the years up to the Second World War. With the symbolism of its emphatic porch and its rustic front gate, it epitomizes our idea of house-and-home, and most British people know its plan backwards.

My grandfather probably adapted both plan and elevations from those published weekly in the *Illustrated Carpenter and Builder*, deposited a plan with the local council, and then got on with building it, at his own pace, between jobs. He died when I was ten and was not interested in housing, so I never had a chance to ask him how it was that in the bad old days any skilled tradesman in the building trades could build himself a house. When I was old enough to ask the right questions I had, like everyone else, read *The Ragged Trousered Philanthropist* and had learned that it was impossible.

However, all through life I have kept hearing of working-class families who *have* managed it, without even building skills, and with little or no access to capital. Everyone today is so completely dependent upon the housing supply system, whether renting in the public sector or buying in the private sector, that we find it hard to believe that people can house themselves. Worse than that, we assume that they are in some way abnormal or obsessional or heroic, so that instead of changing the system to make it easier for others to do the same, we make it harder for anyone to emulate them. Suppose, for the first time in the history of the Left's discussion of housing, we were to celebrate their achievement?

Take the case of Walter Southgate. He, along with Emanuel Shinwell, is one of the two last survivors of the Labour Representation Committee, the body which founded the Labour Party, and for decades was a street-corner agitator and trade-union activist. Later in his long life he was one of the people who established the Museum of Labour History in Limehouse. After the First World War he and his wife bought two and a half acres of land near Ongar in Essex. Back home in Hackney he first made a carpenter's bench and then built in sections a two-roomed wooden hut. Next Easter they hired a Model T Ford van and transported their shed to erect it on the concrete footings they had spent ages building. Their first lesson in brickwork had been in building the fireplace. The four-day holiday gave them time to erect their 8 foot by 16 foot shed and set it up on the footings but not to bolt it down, before it was time to cycle the 20 miles back to Adley Street, opposite Hackney Marshes. That week a gale blew it off its foundations, but they levered it back and used it for several years at weekends while plotting to build a permanent house.

> We knew from the start that it would be a gamble and disastrous should I fall sick or unemployed at a stage when the walls were half way up . . . Our estimate of the cost without labour was around £358 and we had nowhere near that sum. We just hoped to get through the final stages of building our bungalow by working in slow motion on my monthly salary. So it came about a few days before the General Strike was declared in May 1926 that we sent off our first order to the local gravel pits to deliver 30 yards of ballast and 20 yards of sand at 8s a cubic yard. The die had been cast and there could be no going back. It now meant work, hard work, for every weekend and holiday period over the following two and a half years . . .[1]

They finished the building in September 1928 and lived there on the small-holding they developed over the years, until 1955. Over the years they produced every kind of fruit and vegetable, kept poultry, rabbits and geese, grew a variety of trees including a coppice of 650 saplings and in fact made their holding far more productive than any farmer could. Was this a triumph of escapist individualism? Well, not exactly, for Mr Southgate spent a long life in every kind of socialist organization and at the 1978 National Conference was honoured for 'outstanding voluntary service to the Labour Party.'

In the course of our research into the 'plotlands' of South East England,[2] Dennis Hardy and I met dozens of people who, with no capital and no access to mortgage loans, had changed their lives for the better. Mr Fred Nichols of Bowers Gifford had a poverty-stricken childhood in East London and a hard and uncertain living as a casual dock worker. His plot of land, 40 feet wide by 100 feet deep, cost him £10 in 1934. He first put up a tent which his family used at weekends, and then gradually accumulated tools, timber and glass which he brought to the site strapped to his back as he cycled down from London. For water he sank a well in the garden, though as with Mr Southgate's house, main services were eventually connected. His house is called 'Perseverance'.

Mrs Elizabeth Granger and her husband were caretakers in an LCC block of flats. In 1932 she saw in the evening paper land at Laindon advertised at £5 for a plot 20 feet wide by 150 feet deep. She took her unwilling husband on the one-and-twopenny return trip from London and was advised that they should buy two plots if she wanted to build a bungalow. She paid the deposit with a borrowed pound. When she could afford it she bought a First World War army bell tent and laboriously got it to the site. She and her husband would then go there on their day off, taking their drinking water with them and straining rainwater through an old stocking for washing. They used to rent the tent at weekends to parties of boys from the estate, using the money to buy second-hand bricks at 35s a 1,000, three yards of sand for 15s and cement at 2s 6d a bag. They reared chickens, geese and goats, bought a pony and trap, and Mrs Granger's husband got a transfer to a job at Dagenham. Unlike Mr Nichols, they didn't stay for a lifetime in the house they had built with so much labour, but were enabled to move 'up-market' as people would say, from their very modest beginnings – the borrowed pound, in fact. She remarks, 'We never had a mortgage for any of the houses where we have lived. I feel so sorry for young couples these days, who don't get the kind of chance we had.'[3]

The Second World War, and the overwhelming powers to

control development given to planning authorities by the 1947 Town and Country Planning Act and its successors, as well as the stringent enforcement of building regulations, have put an end to this kind of self-help housebuilding in Britain. True, there are people who manage it, but it is not my business to inform on them. We certainly have our self-builders, both individual and collective, and they usually build houses of a much higher quality than they could buy. But they have to provide a fully finished, fully serviced house right from the start. There is no longer any room for the improvised dwelling that is improved from earnings over time, simply because it would not get planning permission, approval under the building regulations, and certainly not a mortgage loan for the cost of the site and materials. A whole new profession has grown up of people who act as 'fixers' for self-build housing groups, simply because of the complexity of the regulations and legal stipulations they have to meet.

Our planning and building legislation, in fact, operates as Jon Gower Davies remarked, as 'a highly regressive form of indirect taxation'.[4] The rich can get by, but the poor are penalized. Contemporary planning legislation would automatically outlaw the building of the homes of Mr Southgate, Mr Nichols and Mrs Granger – it being axiomatic that land in the country is sacrosanct for farmers to grow unwanted cereals for the subsidy, and to pick up another subsidy for grubbing up hedges and trees for this purpose. Contemporary building regulations would certainly ensure that their building costs were prohibitive. Their houses may or may not have been built to the standards of the prewar model bylaws and Public Health Acts. They probably were, since these were simple and comprehensible to the layperson. But the postwar building regulations are not only incomprehensible, so that even architects employ structural engineers, at their client's expense, to design the simplest foundation, beam or roof, but are administered in a way that ensures that all the district council's officers will be insured in perpetuity against the remotest liability for any building failure. Old buildings last for centuries without benefit of all this expertise, while the widespread defects of public housing in the last 20 years, all built to comply with the regulations, turn out to be nobody's responsibility. But if you have the temerity to want to build for yourself, watch out!

Readers who are disinclined to take these comments on trust should ask any architect of their acquaintance. But they may also feel that because the instances I mentioned from years ago are of people who broke out of urban landlordism into the country, I have evaded the issue of those families who from necessity or choice wanted to remain city dwellers, and that of contemporary realities. Postwar housing in the cities has of course been dominated by local authorities, who, presented by the war with bomb sites, adopted the policy of comprehensive redevelopment which fitted their unquestioning belief that large-scale problems could only be met by large-scale solutions. When they ran out of bomb sites they made themselves a second blitz. Colin Jones has shown how the self-confident rush to destroy the past in Glasgow and Liverpool has resulted in a net housing loss[5] and Graham Lomas demonstrated in 1975 how in London more fit houses had been destroyed than had been built since the war.[6]

Two young architects from the London borough of Newham, Graham Bennett and Stuart Rutherford, observed that at a time when the borough was claiming that it had run out of sites, it was, like any other inner-city borough, pockmarked with small vacant plots. They decided to make a detailed investigation. On foot and by bike they surveyed, street by street, two half-kilometre-wide strips of land, from north to south and from west to east, straddling the borough, and noted each vacant site. They then *excluded* all sites of more than half an acre, any sites in wholly industrial areas, any sites which, although not used for anything in particular, were part of recent local authority housing proposals and any sites within a declared local authority redevelopment area.

They concluded on the basis of this survey that, within the borough as a whole, there was enough land in the sites left over to house, at a conservative estimate, 3,000 to 5,000 people in single-family houses. When they reported their findings to officers of the council, they were told that all these small and scattered plots were useless so far as the council was concerned. Given the local authority's procedures, it would be uneconomic to develop them. Bennett and Rutherford were not happy with this answer because they felt, as I do, that the very scale of local authority developments was part of the malaise of public housing. So in 1979 they took their argument further in a detailed report, supported by quantity surveyors' costings.[7] They pointed out that house prices in Newham were below those of neighbouring boroughs. Turn-of-the-century houses were selling for around £9,000, and only reached that figure because of the influx of people who could only just qualify for a mortgage. Consequently, speculative developers could not sell newly built houses at prices which would show what they considered as an adequate return on capital. So the building of new houses was monopolized by local authorities or housing associations.

In consequence, the two architects claimed, 'the considerable contributions which householders can make have never been fully appreciated and utilized.' Public participation has been seen as a politically necessary nuisance or as just another load on administrative costs. But, they argued, 'Until local authorities acknowledge that their bad experiences with participation on large-scale developments have been a product of working on too large a scale, and give consideration to small partnership arrangements for small sites, these sites will remain unusable.' They point out that all the other social needs for land in depressed urban areas – schools, hospitals and recreational open space – *need* large sites. 'The one-family house is, on the other hand, uniquely suited to small sites and is the most intensive use of land. A typical terrace house plot of, say, 15 feet by 70 feet can be, for the family living there, a child's play space, a vegetable garden, a thing of beauty, the site for a hobby or small business, as well as a place of shelter and security. As such it tends to be well cared for and supervised.'

We don't have to look far, they argue, to see how the benefits of small-scale management and enterprise could be harnessed to developing idle sites in depressed districts:

> In all except the coldest winter months, the residential streets of our survey borough are dotted with builders' skips, as local people add a kitchen, bathroom or bedroom to their houses, make a loft conversion, create a 'through lounge' or build on a new front porch. They do so by managing the project themselves, often with the aid of a draughtsman from the local estate agency.

Bennet and Rutherford were putting the case for extending this kind of enterprise to prospective householders. They envisaged a situation where a local authority would be empowered with central government funding to advertise the opportunity to develop these small sites among families on their waiting list for housing. Someone would decide to apply, lease the land at a peppercorn rent, appoint an adviser, and as building work proceeded payments would be made in stages. The council would use its allocation of funds to write off 40 per cent of the capital cost and would grant the low-paid householder an option mortgage for the rest. Their proposal was simply a rearrangement of procedures in a new way, but as they said, 'the greatest impediment to our proposal is simply that many professionals with an interest in, and a controlling hand on, housing have come to believe that housing is a sophisticated process well beyond the comprehension of the uninitiated.'

Needless to say, their scheme was not adopted in Newham.

But the good news is that another London borough has sponsored a scheme which combines their approach with that of the plotland self-builders, *and* has provided housing of high quality giving immense satisfaction to the residents, who claim that the experience has enormously enriched their lives. This is the Lewisham Self-Build Housing Association. As an experiment in dweller-built public housing (something which a decade ago would have sounded like a contradiction in terms) it took a long time to come to fruition, and would have been smothered at birth had it not been for a few people's willingness to put aside the assumptions about the politics of housing which they had accumulated over the years.

Walter Segal is an architect, born in Switzerland in 1907, who quite early in life was fascinated by the structural simplicity and economy of the traditional American 'balloon-framed' timber house. He has practised in this country for almost 50 years, giving a direct personal service to his clients, but has been increasingly at odds with the planning and building control system.

> Whenever a new project came along there was this brief honeymoon with the design, then the long drawn-out fight with the control apparatus. The client had to adjust himself to this. And then there was the final business of building, and there it was harder and harder. When you administer a client's resources you have a moral obligation to him. I built 30 houses in London before 1962 but it was becoming so difficult that it was really warfare – and I had become in consequence a much less amiable person than I am now. I was really quite an unpleasant person to meet professionally.[8]

It was in that year that he decided to rebuild his own house and to erect a temporary building in the garden to house the family during the building work. He used lightweight materials in standard sizes so that they could be reused elsewhere, held together by a simple frame standing on no foundation other than concrete paving slabs. The building was so cheap, quickly built and comfortable (as well as durable: it is still there today) that in the 1960s and 1970s, when the mainstream of British architecture was steadily losing the respect of the public, Segal had a series of commissions to build houses on the same principle in different parts of the country, refining the system with each job. There was no contractor, just a plumber, an electrician and a carpenter, Mr Wade, who followed him around from job to job. An increasing proportion of the building work was being done by the owners.

One of the most interesting aspects of his approach is that it blurs the expected roles of architect, building worker and client. They aren't at the points of a triangular relationship, they are all mixed up in the middle in the adventure of building. 'As I see it,' he says, 'buildings are there to be a background for people, against which they move, a background which envelops them, protects them, gives them pleasure, and allows them to add a little bit of themselves.'[9]

By 1975, having built 25 structures of this kind, Segal was yearning to find a local authority willing to take the plunge and sponsor housing built by his method for and by families on its housing waiting list. At that time the Assistant Borough Architect of Lewisham council was Brian Richardson, seeking alternatives to what he regarded as the failure of the usual, expensive council housing procedures. The chair of the Housing Committee was Ron Pepper, a comprehensive school headmaster, and the chair of the Planning Committee was Nicholas Taylor, author of a brilliant book, *The Village in the City*, who knows a good housing idea when he meets one. Naturally these four people had different responsibilities and different approaches to housing, and of the role of local authorities. Brian Richardson, an anarchist, comments that 'If the Lewisham Labour Group has a fault, it is the conviction that if a thing is worth doing at all, it is worth the council doing it for you.' Taylor on the other hand, speaks of 'Lewisham's libertarian vision of a socialism which is neither of the managerial Right nor of the authoritarian Left, but which uses state intervention to release the creative energies of ordinary people.'[10]

In 1976, by a single vote, Lewisham council decided to explore the possibility of promoting a self-build scheme, based on Segal's system of lightweight construction, for families on the council's waiting or transfer lists, using those pockets of land which because of their size or their sloping nature, could not in their view be used in the borough's own housing programme. The council advertised a public meeting and a lot of people expressed an interest: 168 attended a first meeting, 78 a second, and finally 14 families were successful in a draw for places for the first scheme. 'They were a miscellaneous bunch of ordinary south Londoners who were alike only in their passionate desire to escape from their present housing conditions . . . into something that would make their lives more generous and free . . .'[11]

There followed two and a half years of delay, enough to dishearten the most persistent of would-be builders. The scheme was 'totally entangled in a complicated bureaucratic maze through conflicting demands by local authorities and the government', it was reported in August 1978. It took five months to obtain planning permission and further difficulty arose with the GLC and the District Surveyor because of the unorthodox structure. The families formed themselves into an association, and in order to qualify for subsidy, they contracted to build the houses for the council which would then grant them 99-year leases and 50 per cent mortgages. The other 50 per cent of the house would be 'rented' from the council but would be purchaseable in instalments to enable the residents eventually to own the whole property. The value of the labour in building the houses would be assessed and set against the mortgage.

This ingenious scheme survived with difficulty, as first the DOE demanded as a condition of loan sanction that there should be a fixed price and fixed time contract, and secondly the Inland Revenue demanded that the self-builders should be taxed at the standard rate for their labour as though it were income. During the long period of waiting, the members taught themselves to build. Walter Segal recalls,

> An evening school was arranged which ran for six months to show them how to use very simple tools. It was mainly cutting, drilling and measuring. What was so utterly astonishing was the patience, the incredible patience which these people displayed in waiting so long for an opportunity to get on the site. In the end even the council thought it was expecting too much and it was mainly Ron Pepper who said he would take it on himself to let them go and clear the site; and later on he authorized the first two houses to be done.[12]

Although they were using Segal's precisely calculated structural system the internal design of each house was determined by each family. As Ken Atkins explains,

> We must be the first council tenants who have been involved with an architect in the design of our own homes. The architect used graph paper to help us get it to represent the modular concept of 2 feet 2 inches and asking us to draw a house within cash limits. This was about 100 square metres. We did this as a group and then went to Walter Segal's house. He took all the ideas and drew up 50 to 60 different house plans and then we went back as individual families to choose and adapt our design . . . Every wall is non-loadbearing so it's adaptable and changeable. At any time during the process of building, after I've lived in it, if I feel I want to change it I can take out any wall and change it.[13]

Anyone who has seen a videotape of the 'Open Door' TV programme about Lewisham, *The House that Mum and Dad Built*, (the BBC2 presentation brought over 1,000 enquiries) will have been struck by the members' testimony about the effect that this adventure has had on their lives:

> The one thing that's left me immensely proud is the co-operative spirit on the Brockley site. A wife had a baby the other week. The buntings were out and the balloons . . . If someone requires a babysitter . . . if someone's working on a car . . . or the communal garden . . . they get help. They pay a pound a week to a communal fund. They've landscaped the gardens last year. No-one tells them to do that, they do it themselves because they have control over where they are living and they contribute. They've got a say in what actually goes on there and because they have a say they contribute . . .

For the professionals involved it was an equally liberating experience. Brian Richardson says it was the most important architectural experience of his life, and Walter Segal, an old man who has seen a dozen architectural fashions come and go, says, 'On the day when the first frame stood it was an astonishing feeling. I was immensely happy, like a child, almost.'

Many self-build housing schemes organized in a conventional way rely, believe it or not, on a system of penalties in case some member does not pull his or her weight. Segal recalls the creativity that was revealed in Lewisham by *not* pushing people around!

> Help was to be provided mutually and voluntarily – there were no particular constraints on that, which did mean that the good will of people could find its way through. The less you tried to control them the more you freed the element of good will – this was

astonishingly clear. Children were of course expected and allowed to play on the site. And the older ones also helped if they wished to help. That way one avoided all forms of friction. Each family were to build at their own speed and within their own capacity. We had quite a number of young people but some that were 60 and over also managed to build their own houses . . . They were told that I would not interfere with the internal arrangement. I let them make their own decisions, therefore we had no difficulties.

He noted with pleasure rather than with irritation, the 'countless small variations and innovations and additions' that the self-builders made. 'It is astonishing that there is among the people that live in this country such a wealth of talent.'[14]

All this fuss about 14 houses! Why has it not been followed up elsewhere, apart from a second Lewisham scheme where, working with John Broome, Segal is supervising another tenant group building 13 more? The answer is in the inflexibility of the housing supply system which was never designed to liberate that astonishing wealth of talent. In Scotland, Stirling District Council is proposing to adopt a scheme devised by Rod Hackney for a serviced plot system where ground-floor slabs with service ducts through the slabs will be poured and the individual sites then sold to self-builders. The Housing Committee chair says that the council 'would do everything possible to assist potential owners to arrange mortgages, and in certain cases the council might be prepared to give a loan themselves.'[15]

But, even in 1984, many Labour councillors still share the view of the leader of another London council when he concluded his visit to Lewisham, 'We're not going to turn *our* tenants into little capitalists.'

6. Rediscovering co-operation

> The most important thing about it is the power to the people bit. In general; in Liverpool people are told what they are getting, not asked what they want. But once we had established our viability by being accepted by the government for funding, we determined everything; the way we lived, and who we employed to run our affairs. We did not succumb to bureaucracy.
>
> We got the architects and builders and everybody else on our terms. We told them what we wanted and consulted right the way through, from day one, at every stage. Through the design committee we decided on every single aspect of the scheme right down to the sort of trees we planted.
>
> We've proved to the council and government and anybody else listening that if people are given the reins, get the right help and are committed, they can come up with a really excellent viable housing scheme that people *want* to live in.
>
> Alan Hoyte, first Chair of Hesketh Street
Co-operative, 1984.

Years ago members of housing committees and housing managers used to go on guided tours to admire Scandinavian housing, though they seldom took any tenants. Their hosts would explain, 'Of course, we owe it all to your Rochdale Pioneers.' For they assumed that since the co-operative movement originated in Britain, we must have developed co-operative housing here as an automatic application of the co-operative principle. In fact the evolution of any kind of tenant participation in housing management, let alone co-operative control or ownership, has been confined to the last 15 years.

Council housing grew up in a period when building was cheap, simple and durable, not plagued with condensation and maintenance problems, when it was occupied by respectful, regularly paid small earners (never the poorest of the poor) and administered and cared for by rent collectors who would give advice on hygiene and floor scrubbing and caretakers with a background of the armed forces who kept everything shipshape. Kenneth Campbell, former Principal Housing Architect for the LCC, told me that the decline of the council's estates was simultaneous with the decline of the Royal Navy: all those former stokers and chief petty officers who needed a berth ashore for themselves and knew how to maintain a happy ship. The GLC filled the gap they had left with 'mobile caretakers' and the one thing that a mobile caretaker won't do is to take care.

There were always voices warning that paternalism couldn't go on for ever. I have already mentioned the nice irony that it is exactly a century since Beatrice Webb (who we usually associate with a managerial rather than a participatory interpretation of socialism) remarked, 'The idea of developing self-government among the tenants has to be gradually introduced.' By the 1940s a Political and Economic Planning report on *Councils and their Tenants* was observing that

> The council itself is sometimes resented as an omnipresence controlling almost every aspect of the tenants' lives. They feel that it is impossible for them to escape its tentacles; it controls not only the routine services which local authorities were originally established to provide, but also the schools to which the

children go, the clinics and health centres, the community centre in which the tenants amuse themselves, and finally the houses in which they live.[1]

And by the early 1960s Stanley Alderson was warning that

The private tenant can at least hate his landlord for taking advantage of the conditions of shortage for his own financial gain. The council tenant knows that he is fortunate in having his house, and feels that he has been done a favour. The local authority which is his landlord never does anything for its own financial gain. It always acts in its wisdom for its tenants' own advantage. In the long run, power employed paternalistically provokes far greater resentment than power employed selfishly or even antagonistically. Because there is no satisfactory outlet for it the resentment accumulates . . .[2]

This kind of warning was not merely unheeded, it was also regarded as mischievous by the oligarchy of councillors, housing managers and architects who had exclusive and monopolistic access to public funds for housing in the postwar decades. We all know the dreadful and expensive saga of the tower block era, though in the miasma of self-deception of socialist housing polemics, we attribute that particular disaster to the capitalist contractors who made money out of it, rather than to the Labour councils and progressive architects who employed them. But towers are the spectacular tip of the iceberg. When architectural fashion suggested low-rise maisonettes, the tenants' response has been the same. They call their blocks Alcatraz or the Gulag or Casablanca, because they are reminded of the vernacular architecture of penology or the forts of the French Foreign Legion.

Take note of the obituary, written by Alison Ravetz for Hunslet Grange:

The life of council estates gets shorter all the time. Hunslet Grange, built on the Yorkshire Development Group (YDG) system, is to be demolished at an age of barely 14 years . . . The tenants tried to meet the council to discuss the damp and other problems within months of the flats opening in 1968. The council did not want to listen . . . The few outsiders who visit Hunslet Grange can hardly credit its grey monotony, desolate street decks, turf mounds of rubble labelled 'play spaces' and its level of vandalism. They would be more incredulous if they knew that the glossy brochure announcing its opening described its layout as 'villages' and that its architect, Martin Richardson, has drawn parallels between the design and the Yorkshire vernacular with its intimacy and sudden vistas.[3]

The same kind of grotesque architectural self-deception survived the period of vast estates. Suddenly the architects and chairs of housing committees began to talk about 'intimate, high-density, low-rise housing'. When ITV's 'World in Action' visited Liverpool in the spring of 1984 to ask why, in a city with 22,000 people on the housing waiting list there were 20,000 council houses empty, one of the places described as uninhabitable by its tenants was a 'seven-year-old estate modelled on a Cornish fishing village.'[4]

In the new city of Milton Keynes there is a quite measurable scale by which housing is assessed by tenants. At the most disliked end of the scale comes the housing by the most prestigious architects, the leaders of their profession. The most sought after is that which most resembles the traditional image of house-and-home, with a pitched roof and a chimney on top, and a front porch with roses round the door. This of course, was most despised by the professionals of design.

But the argument for dweller control is not about design:

it is about who decides. The Lewisham self-build houses are uncompromisingly 'modern' and even have flat roofs, since that enabled them to be built without the use of scaffolding. In any case most of us live in houses or flats which were there long before we were. The point is that the worst of our housing errors and follies would never have occurred if popular preferences had been heeded. The argument for housing co-operatives is that it is a mode of tenure which changes the situation of dependency to one of independence, that it is one which, as the veteran co-operative advocate Harold Campbell put it years ago, 'combines private enterprise and mutual aid in a unique form of social ownership which puts a premium on personal responsibility and individual initiative.'[5]

It is remarkable how hostile the housing establishment has been towards this worthy aim. When I had the opportunity of addressing the annual conference of the Housing Centre Trust in 1974, setting out my views on the need to transfer the control of municipal housing from councils to tenants, I was greeted (according to a full and fair report in the *Municipal Journal*) 'with astonishment and disbelief in most quarters'. And when, that year, in my book, *Tenants Take Over*, I sought to describe a precedent, I had to turn to Oslo as the nearest example. A decade later we have a number of examples closer to home, including instances of how *not* to go about it. It is really astonishing how the political Left feels threatened by the advocacy of housing co-ops. I was invited in 1975 to address a public meeting organized by the Co-operative Party in the London Borough of Wandsworth where I then lived. John Hands and I, as advocates of co-operative housing, were met with bitter antagonism not by the audience, but by the Co-operative chairperson, who at that time was also chair of our local Housing Committee, and by, of all people, the then Political Secretary of the London Co-operative Society.

At that time we actually had a Minister for Housing, Reg

Freeson, who was the only occupant of that office to understand what co-operative housing was all about and why it was important for socialists. He rebuked those members of his own party who sneered in the usual way that co-operative housing was a bit of trendy middle-class self-interest by pointing out that the most successful co-operatives were those whose members were very poor tenants of housing taken over from private landlords in Liverpool, or actually homeless people who housed themselves through the Holloway Tenant Co-operative in London. He also set up in 1976 a Co-operative Housing Agency to serve the functions of what is known in co-operative theory as a tertiary co-operative until the co-operative housing movement was strong enough to support its own. But his own government closed it down again in November 1978, its functions reverting to the Housing Corporation. During its lifetime only 72 housing co-operatives had been registered with the agency. Harold Campbell asks why anyone was surprised:

> Co-operation is a learning process. Education and training is a basic requirement which is labour-intensive and time-consuming, particularly in the gestation period following any new co-operative conception. New ideas, in housing tenure no less than in retail business ownership and control, take time to get established. Even longer if they uproot all the concepts that have preceded them.[6]

By now there are several hundred housing co-operatives with many thousands of members, certainly a rate of growth faster than that in the first three-quarters of this century. They have a fascinating variety of origins, from the 'legitimization of squatters' groups, such as the Seymour Co-op in West London (the product of endless bargaining with the housing authority for derelict property), and the Stephen and Matilda Co-op in South London, to the very exciting 'new-build' co-operatives in Liverpool.

The pioneers of co-operative housing at a local level have had to fight hard all the way to make the official system of the control of housing and of its finance work in ways that meet their needs. Tony Gibson, who has put a lot of effort into identifying the factors which make for success in this kind of community enterprise, stresses the importance of shared pleasure in cementing the bonds of neighbourhood solidarity:

> Many inside the bureaucracy live out their working lives insulated from close contact with the people affected by their administrative decisions. They tend to assume that 'the residents' don't really understand what is needed, let alone what is practicable. Recently, as they neared the completion of their new housing, the Weller Streets Co-operative went to see the City Engineer to discuss their plans for landscaping the spaces between the houses. They were confronted with a simple choice – tarmac, red or green. It took them many months to get across the simple fact of community life; a group which has the decisive hand in planning its own environment seldom suffers vandalism. So flowers, shrubs, grass and trees can be planted to give each cluster of houses its own individuality; and what is planted will thrive . . . The 'happening' which literally underlay the Weller Streets landscaping activities took place when the co-operative celebrated taking over the bare site with a fancy dress party in the open air, in the course of which besides making their own refreshments and sharing them with the surrounding residents, they got out pick axes and a pneumatic drill and started to salvage and sort out the cobbles and the slabs of York stone buried beneath the rubble. It is only when everyone can join in, planning the garden space and the kitchen layout, stacking the cobbles, cutting the sandwiches, humping the tea urn and the

beer – that the credit for what happens and the
satisfaction that results, can be truly shared. This
collective job satisfaction spreads and sustains local
initiative. It is the crucial ingredient which turns a
mixture of many different people into a compound
with its own properties and its own staying power.[7]

He is telling more than a cosy human story, for he is describing how a successful co-operative works. The dozen or so housing co-ops that grew up in Liverpool in the 1970s to take over from private landlords have deliberately kept their membership numbers well below 100 each, precisely because 'Once a co-operative gets too large, decision making appears to become too complicated and ordinary members begin to feel out of touch with their elected committee.'[8] When they get too big they divide. The same point is made by one of the secondary co-operatives, Solon Co-operative Housing Services, which was itself devolved from Solon Housing Association and has recently divided itself in two, serving primary co-operatives in North and East London. 'Even early on we recognized that size might at some point impede the very co-operative working methods we were striving to pioneer in the housing field.'[9]

It is from Liverpool that there has come the development that Nick Wates claims to be the most important step forward in British housing for decades: newly built housing, funded by the council, but developed by the prospective residents. He explained in 1982 that

Liverpool City Council no longer uses its own
architect's department to build, on spec, new public
housing for rent – apart from a small amount for
special needs. Instead it funds the people who need
new housing to organize the design, construction and
management of it themselves through self-generating
self-reliant co-operatives.

Liverpool's first new-build co-operative scheme for

61 houses was funded by the Housing Corporation and is now two-thirds occupied. Nine more, involving 341 families, have been approved and are at various stages of design and construction, and several more are in the pipeline. All but one are being financed by the city council.

It works like this. Local authority tenants living in slum clearance areas or deteriorating tenements organize themselves into groups – so far ranging from 19 to 61 family units – and obtain the management services of one of Liverpool's co-operative development agencies: Co-operative Development Services, Merseyside Improved Houses or Neighbourhood Housing Services. With its assistance they register as a 'non-equity' housing co-operative with limited liability, locate a suitable site and negotiate to buy it. (So far nearly all the land has come from Liverpool City Council or the Merseyside Development Corporation.) They then select a firm of architects with whom they design a scheme which is submitted to a funding body. The scheme is then submitted to the DOE for subsidy and yardstick approval as on all local authority funded housing association schemes. When the houses are built, the co-op members become the tenants of their homes, paying standard fair rents, but they are also collectively the landlord, responsible for management and maintenance.[10]

The first, and most famous, of the new co-ops, Weller Streets, was followed by the Hesketh Street Co-op, where once again the members are low-income families from poor housing, including pensioners and unemployed people who are eloquent about the way in which being involved in their own housing has changed their lives. 'It's to do with caring. People got to know each other during the design stage and we agreed things together. I feel I've known everybody now all my life,' one member explained to Hugh Anderson who made an independent appraisal of the scheme for the *Architects' Journal*. He concluded by asking, 'Why is it that so little housing design is done on the Hesketh Street basis?' His answer was,

> I fear that the major reason is inertia. Users, designers and bureaucrats have not stopped to solve the problem. There are fears about its uncontrollability and its costs. These have been shown to be either unfounded, or in the interests of the quality of the product that can be produced, set against the countless other social costs that poor design and housing provision currently result in. In asking whether we can afford such a method of working, we should ask whether we can afford not to have it – especially in a time of limited funds.[11]

Very slowly a few local authorities, including some with past records of heavy-handed paternalism towards their tenants, have been resolving to put the modernization of council houses and flats in the hands of the occupiers. Jeremy Seabrook has described in fascinating detail the decentralization of housing services when the new breed of Labour councillors took office in the metropolitan borough of Walsall in May 1980, only to be ousted two years later by a Conservative-Liberal 'anti-socialist coalition'. Needless to say the first thing that happened to Walsall's 'left-wing Tribune triad' was a confrontation with NALGO, and the most telling of Seabrook's anecdotes is about the debt-counselling officer who suggested to a woman who bought two packets of chips for her children that she could have saved 20p by making do with one. The highly decentralized Debt Counsellor earned £9,000 a year from the council. And here is the appalling difficulty about the expensive business of looking after people. They would be better off if they simply had the cash to look after themselves.

Dave Church, the former chair of housing, told Seabrook about the discussions in the period leading up to Labour's taking office. 'At this time I had the dream of co-operatives. I thought we could arrange it so that the whole of an estate would be completely free to run itself, nothing to do with the council. The idea of people determining their own plans was already there. We had some wild and wonderful schemes . . .'[12]

But there is nothing wild and wonderful about extending to council tenants that degree of self-determination which is taken for granted by the majority of households in this country. Glasgow city council sought to put rehabilitation in the hands of tenants through its 'tenant's grant scheme', taken up by more than 10,000 of the city's tenants, 96 per cent of those to whom it was offered, and the result, according to Jane Morton, 'startled even those who argued for it in 1979 by its cost-effectiveness and popularity.'[13] Subsequent developments in Glasgow have been even more significant. Glasgow's problems are of course very like those of Merseyside and the council had noted the decision to turn over the Cantril Farm estate outside Liverpool to a private developer to retrieve at least something from the wreck of past housing policies. Glasgow's Housing Convenor, Jim Maclean, desperately looking for a way of using the dwindling sums allocated by central government for modernization, says, 'I think that we've found a socialist answer to Cantril Farm.' This is how Jane Morton describes the latest Glasgow proposals:

> Before the year is out, around 1,000 Glasgow council tenants – very few of whom could have contemplated buying their own house – will have bought the estates they live on, collectively, under the city's unique new 'community ownership' scheme. More than a quarter of the city's 180,000 tenants could ultimately own their homes under this scheme. Estates which wish to take

part begin by forming what is known in Scotland as a par value co-operative. It costs tenants £1 to join. The co-op as a separate legal entity then negotiates a purchase price with the city. In most cases, all further costs are likely to be charged to members as a cost rent – as with a cost-rent housing society. This is to protect tenants' entitlement to housing benefit. Over 60 per cent of Glasgow's tenants currently receive housing benefit. But some may feel able to go for co-ownership arrangements, which would allow them to claim a share in the value of the estate if they have to move.

Glasgow came to 'community ownership' in January, at the end of a search for some way of upgrading its 1950s estates . . . The city's estate modernization programme was due to reach these homes in about three years, once 25,000 earlier homes had been dealt with. Then the Scottish Office abruptly altered the balance of Glasgow's capital allocation . . . Only if they could be shifted bodily into another sector, Glasgow concluded, would these estates now see modernization within the decade. There was some doubt at first that enough tenants would wish to join their neighbours in a co-op. But the first four estates approached, all from the 1950s, have jumped at the chance.[14]

The city council in Glasgow has also jumped at the chance to move into the tenant takeover just because of the vagaries of central government funding. (The sum the city has been allowed to spend in 1984–5 on its own housing has been reduced from £72 million to £49 million, while the sum allocated to other sectors, which house a third of the population was increased from £54 million to £77 million.) The council has simply made the best of the situation. But it has had experience of the day-to-day problems with council-sponsored co-ops from its experiment in sponsoring the Summerston management co-op in new housing in the late

1970s. It had its ups and downs but surmounted them. 'The best proof of this recovery is that tenants in other parts of Summerston, who in earlier days had rejected the idea of forming co-ops, have changed their minds.'[15]

In Liverpool, however, co-operatives were not regarded by Labour councillors as a socialist answer to the privatization that the council had found the only solution to the Everton Piggeries or that the neighbouring council had adopted as a rescue job for Cantril Farm. For it was the Liberal regime in the city which (acting upon Reg Freeson's circular of 1976) had sponsored the new co-operatives like Weller Streets and Hesketh Street. In May 1983, at a 'stormy and heavily pre-election meeting', the then ruling Liberals had Conservative support in voting for a policy of adopting a co-operative approach to 'the city's much-troubled estates at Croxteth and Gillmoss, where residents and community groups will be asked to discuss with officers and councillors the formation of co-operatives to take over the management of their estates.'[16]

The council elections that month gave Labour control of the city. One of the new council's first decisions was to withdraw the funding (with DOE cash) of eight co-ops (509 houses) which had been in preparation for two years. This was of course sharply criticized by the other political parties and bitterly attacked by the co-op members. Two of the co-ops succeeded in getting funding from an alternative source, the Housing Corporation. The chair of the Housing Committee then proposed to each of the others 'that the council take over their projects, keep the present architects and build the houses to the tenant's designs. But they would then be let as normal council tenancies managed by the direct labour department.'[17] According to the *New Statesman*, 'since the offer, letters from the co-ops have not been answered, and offers of alternative housing have been made in what seems like a cynical attempt at attrition, so far without success.'[18]

A member of the Luke Street Co-op commented on the council's decision, 'We've proved that working-class people can design and build their homes. They just don't *want* us to have any control.'

7. Leavening the Lump

Unemployment in the building industry has rocketed to 400,000.
Labour Housing Group, *Right to a Home*, page 18.

300,000 building workers are unemployed
Labour Housing Group, *Right to a Home*, page 60.

Don't think I'm laughing at the authors of the 1984 'radical blueprint' for housing or at their inability to decide how many building workers are out of work. Nobody has any idea. The monthly unemployment figures issued by the Department of Employment are just as misleading as the criminal statistics issued by the Home Office, and are an equally unreliable guide to what is happening in the real world. For apart from the usual notorious inaccuracies, hundreds of thousands of building workers are self-employed, so that when they are seeking work they are not registered as unemployed. Nor, of course, are they entitled to draw unemployment benefit.

What I would *like* to believe about all those 'unemployed' building workers is that they are busy in the informal economy, doing for neighbours and local contacts all those repairs and renovation jobs that are so urgently needed, so all reports tell us, in both the owner-occupation and the council house sides of town. (For, whether the tenancy agreement puts the responsibility onto tenants or not, a vast amount of redecoration and modernization is done by tenants, either themselves or by paying someone to do the job.[1])

Do-it-yourself is Britain's biggest industry, even though its enormous output doesn't figure in the calculation of the Gross Domestic Product, except in terms of the booming sale of materials by builders' merchants and ironmongers. A thousand handbooks, evening classes, radio and TV programmes have demystified the techniques of building and household servicing among householders, and people who lack the time, skill or inclination to do it themselves, obviously turn not to a contracting firm with its large overheads, but to a neighbour, relation, friend or word-of-mouth contact to do the job for them. This is natural and desirable and is part of that reciprocal network of mutual services that holds society together. By now it is only people with a singularly authoritarian view of the way the system works who could stigmatize normal human behaviour as the 'black' economy. In 1984 the Chancellor of the Exchequer chose to express his contempt for the way poor people live by imposing VAT on take-away food and in the same budget did his best to turn us all into criminals by imposing 15 per cent VAT on alteration and improvement building work, without even consulting the civil servants in the Department of the Environment on the implications of this measure for poor people struggling to maintain their homes.

People who feel conscientious qualms about paying for building services rendered in cash, because they feel that they are somehow defrauding the social services, should reflect that the British taxpayer is committed to paying around £3 million a day in maintaining a military presence in the Falkland Islands, and that in the sharing of this and all the other tax burdens, the after-tax income of the top 1 per cent of the population rose by 75 per cent in the first three years of office of the Thatcher government, while that of the bottom 50 per cent of the population rose by only 41 per cent. If they are in that particular minority whose income has catastrophically declined in the last five years, they should be all the more thankful for the existence of an area of the building industry which actually attunes itself to their needs. Other people should remind themselves that the existence of the 'black' economy, totally unknown in our parents' day, is entirely the creation of the revenue departments and should consider its advantages practically, not morally.

The practical advantages of the informal economy in the building trades have been set out by two authors whose aim was simply to consider the opportunities for self-employment among the young. Richard Bourne and Jessica Gould remark that,

> it is not only their comparative cheapness that makes services offered in the informal economy so attractive. They are more flexible, too. In households where everyone is out all day at work or school, it can be well nigh impossible because much of the formal sector closes shop in the evenings and at weekends. People working in the informal economy are less likely to be so rigid – they want all the work they can get. . . . Workers in the black economy often do not operate fixed rates, either: they may reduce their charges for little old ladies and add on a little extra when working for the better-off. People employed in the formal economy have no such option: their employer fixes the rate for the job and if the customer can't afford to pay that rate, the work is not done . . . There is thus a semi-voluntary quality about work in the informal economy. The people doing the work are paid in cash, and on piece rates. Those who employ them do so when they want work done, and at the rate for which they have money to pay them. The worker does a job when he [sic] has time, or need of

money, and not if he doesn't. Work is less coercive,
and the deal more like one struck between friends. If
the customer wants something done quickly, it can be.
If he is short of money, the job can be stretched out
over a period of time, with the worker doing the job
one night a week, and being paid as he goes along . . .

If he is bad at his job he will get no work, so he has
to be jealous of his reputation for quality and
reliability. All this means that the customer often has
greater power over the services offered to him by the
informal economy than he does over those in the
formal sector, where faceless bureaucracies make the
decisions on prices, quality and availability of services,
and everything is much more standardized . . . A
householder, wanting alterations, may find a builder
who is prepared to do the work for weekly cash
payments. VAT is not paid, and so the job is slightly
cheaper for both parties. The householder, builder and
architect can meet regularly to discuss the progress of
the work, iron out any problems and ensure that the
work is done to the required standard: because
the work is paid for on a piecework basis, substandard work will not be accepted and so there is an
immediacy of responsibility on the part of the
contractor to the customer which is rarely matched in
the formal economy.[2]

This is so accurate a description of transactions that have
being going on for centuries: ever since wandering bands of
building tradesmen built the medieval cathedrals in fact,
that I for one, cannot take seriously the idea that this direct
relationship between tradesman and customer could possibly
be seen as illegal or undesirable. It's the system that has gone
wrong, not us. But the arguments that have been going on
for decades between the various parties in the building
industry have not been about service to the dweller at all,

they have been about two different conceptions of the builder's role, about DLO and the Lump.

The initials DLO refer to Direct Labour Organizations maintained by local authorities to do their building work, and they have, needless to say, been the subject of political battle for decades, over the heads of the people actually employed. Direct Labour is, of course, an obvious target for the Conservative government, locally or nationally, just as it has become a kind of utopia for people who believe that municipal is best. Trying to be fair, let's say that wages are low but regular, conditions are good – everything that the unions ever demanded,[3] but that, from the point of view of tenants DLO is just something to be put up with. Back in the 1970s Tom Forester was reporting that 'only one in seven of DLO manpower is engaged on new building. The rest are engaged on routine maintenance and conversion work which mostly accounts for the "dirty work" image of DLOs. It also saps morale.'[4] But it saps the morale of the tenants rather more, with the grotesque situation I have quoted from David Blunkett, a believer in Direct Labour, of 'workers and tenants hating each other.' This could never be the position of householder and builder freely negotiating a job of work, but is, I fear, characteristic of the way maintenance is organized. The team brought in to stimulate community-based improvement programmes on inner London housing estates, was obliged to report that 'One of our most difficult tasks was penetrating the bureaucracy of the GLC maintenance department (now London Community Builders) and obtaining a suitable and adequate response.'[5]

At the opposite pole from council Direct Labour is the Lump, which for 20 years has been the focus of equally intense political argument. The term has been used indiscriminately to describe a variety of forms of work organization, some of them very old indeed, some with very ugly features, and some with very desirable aspects. It implies labour-only subcontracting, and covers the small specialist subcontractor with a handful of employees, the self-employed gang of specialists like tilers, pilers or steeplejacks, gangs of similarly self-employed workers recruited by an outsider for a particular job, or simply individual tradesmen or labourers hiring their services for one job after another.

As the Lump grew in the building boom of the 1960s a curious coalition grew up to oppose it and to demand legislation outlawing it. A former building worker, Dave Lamb, concluded that if the government, the employers and the building unions were hostile to it, there must be something in it for the workers. He was not wrong, but found how firmly entrenched in the traditional Left was the opposition to the idea of workers taking their livelihoods into their own hands when he published his pamphlet 'The Lump: an heretical analysis' in 1974. Here he examined one by one the objections raised to the existence of the Lump: accusations like jerry-building, scab labour, high accident rate and so on and found them to be untrue. He was not a defender of the Lump, but he concluded that 'The real threat which the Lump poses is one of *control*: lump workers at present, cannot be controlled,'[6] and in replying to his critics, he reiterated this point, commenting that 'It is *precisely* this lack of *control* that unites employers, union officials and taxmen in opposition to the Lump. The prospect of an entire section of the working class out of control is a nightmare that must haunt those whose claim to power is bound up with institutions committed to the management of others.'[7]

Ironically, the Lump in one of its forms, that of the autonomous group of self-employed workers contracting to do a particular job and organizing it among themselves, is the nearest form of work organization we are likely to see to that recommended by 'experts' to the Institute of Building. Its publication on motivations tells contractors that their attitude to building workers is based on outmoded theories that see workers as 'typically lazy, dishonest, aimless, dull and above all mercenary'. The author, Anthony Mason, tells builders that 'money is *not* the only factor which determines employee performance. Equity of pay, group influences and individual need differences are just as important,' and reminds them that 'higher levels of productivity and worker satisfaction could then be gained through a policy which makes the operative feel wanted, appreciated and respected, and by allowing him to participate in planning his work.'[8]

I have never heard of a building firm that operated these principles, but it can happen in some forms of labour-only subcontracting in the same way as it happened in the 'gang' system once worked in some of the Coventry engineering firms[9] or in the 'composite work' system of the old Durham coalmines,[10] where a group of workers contracted jointly to carry out a contract in what was in effect a workers' co-operative. A variety of attempts have been made at one time or another to put workers' control into practice in the building industry, and the most interesting was the development of Building Guilds under the influence of the guild socialist movement at the end of the First World War. Raymond Postgate summed up its significance in one sentence, with a sting in its tail: 'Perhaps the most important achievement of the Guild was that it gave the workers of the building industry confidence and showed them that they were competent to run and control the industry, if only they could lay their hands on it.'[11]

On the other hand, chastened by failure, we might very well conclude that if workers can't control the industry, they can very well control their part in it. House building and renovation is a labour-intensive occupation that experience tells us is at its best on a small and local scale. Our housing failures were built by the giant contractors using sophisticated plant and large-scale methods, as well as a labour organization which denied any responsibility to building tradespeople. Our housing successes were built by a host of two-men-and-a-boy businesses, grossly undercapitalized, with a bankruptcy every week. Take the interwar boom in suburban housing.

The notion that it was 'jerry-built' is slightly absurd when compared with the record of postwar building. Nor was the typical builder remotely like the cartoonist's plutocrat. A few big contracting firms were involved, but most of the big builders did not make their fortunes until the period was over, when they were involved in those incredibly lucrative wartime airfield contracts on a cost-plus basis. Most of the 4,000,000 suburban houses built between the wars in the private sector were built by 76,112 small firms.

Even the subsequent plutocrats of the industry started on what must sound today like an absurdly small scale. Frank Taylor of Taylor Woodrow built his first pair of houses when he was 16. He had £30, his father had £70 and he persuaded the manager of the District Bank to lend him £400. Two years later he had to take his uncle, Frank Woodrow, into partnership as his solicitor discovered that he was under age. I mention this, not to praise Taylor Woodrow, but to illustrate the fact that there is no magical expertise involved in the ancient art of house building.

In the last decade we have rediscovered the virtues of workers' co-operatives in the building trade. The best-known of them, Sunderlandia Ltd, has failed and the reasons for its failure are instructive.[12] But houses got built, nothing was lost except illusions, and a lot of people benefited from the experience. A number of other building co-operatives manage to make a living for their members, often in such a small way that the word co-operative is a little pretentious for the scale on which they operate. Rose, a builder, was unemployed and joined a small group who set up a limited company to do house repairs.

> Then some more people got involved and it became more of a co-operative and started to settle down. People began to specialize in certain areas so you did actually begin to learn things, you were doing things more than once. It was on a local basis, commercial.

People would come in and say, 'I've got the papers from the council and I want you to do my improvement grant.' We'd take it in turns to follow up a job, doing the paperwork, making sure the drawings got done and were sent in, doing the estimate, and negotiating with the client and running the actual building job. That went on for about three years.[13]

She remained self-employed, working as a carpenter, but 'would really like to work in a co-operative again.' This small-scale, day-to-day way of working is largely dependent on the wild fluctuations of government policy on improvement grants, just as the whole building industry has for years been at the mercy of stop-go economic policy.

But at the neighbourhood level, it is the natural way of getting things done, blurring the distinctions between builder and client and between do-it-yourself and professional work. I mentioned that I would *like* to believe that all those 'unemployed' building workers were picking up a living this way, but my optimism is probably misplaced. Such research findings as we have suggest that informal work, 'as the most rapidly growing type of employment does not necessarily help those households in which there are no earners and who most want to work.' Ray Pahl stresses that 'working informally requires more than just time: tools, materials and travel are all expensive'; in other words that those local and informal building activities are more likely to be done by moonlighters than by unemployed people.[14] This is not an argument against the importance of the informal economy, it is an argument for spreading its benefits to those for whom the official economy has no use and whose lives are so close to the subsistence margin that they can't pick themselves off the industrial scrap heap without aid. As it is, they are both condemned to idleness and simultaneously stigmatized as scroungers. In the British system of supplementary benefits any earnings over £4 a week are deducted from benefit, while earnings of over £2 a day are deducted from unemployment benefit. Professor Jonathan Bradshaw reports that 'we are almost unique among European countries in the severity of the work test in our assistance scheme.'[15] Two simple measures would do more to change the situation of unemployed building workers than massive public works schemes put in the hands of the big contractors. They are the lifting of the earnings threshold for claimants, and tax concessions to enable small building co-ops to get off the ground.

8. Do we need a plan?

> The association estimates that almost £25 billion is needed to repair all the substandard housing stock in England; another £10 billion is needed to put right design defects, and £15 billion to meet the shortage of housing in Britain. That is a total bill for both private and public sectors of £50 billion – the equivalent of about £1,000 for every man, woman and child in the country.
> Association of Metropolitan Authorities' submission to Inquiry into British Housing, September 1984.

At one of those conferences on the problems of our cities where the well-paid and secure sit around discussing the problems of the poor and insecure, Ray Pahl identified six contrasting approaches to urban issues. The participants in these discussions, he noted, could be divided between,

1. Those who believe in the 'technological fix'. They are the Whitehall and local authority executives who see themselves as the preeminent providers of services and facilities, with a heavy emphasis on professional and managerial skills.
2. The political radicals who believe that the professionals are engaged in a conspiracy against the public for their own aggrandisement. They further believe that nothing can be solved without changing the whole system.
3. The populist, anarchist apoliticals who also believe in

the conspiracy of the professionals, but who declare that people can and should do something now.
4. Those who share the mistrust of the professionals, but see answers in the arts, crafts and community work, declaring that small is beautiful.
5. The pragmatic realists who know in their practical hearts that in the end piecemeal amelioration will be called in to do the job.
6. The one-off fixers whose approach is: bring in the consultants, sort out priorities, put a figure and a time limit to the job and then throw in the task force.

For politicians and administrators, the first and last of these categories are naturally the favoured approaches. All my life politicians of all parties have been conducting crusades against slum housing and declaring their intention to treat their attack on the housing problem as a military operation. But success has always eluded them and many of the measures they have taken to make the situation better have in fact made it worse. In the 40 years since the end of the Second World War, we have experienced the 'technological fix' and a whole succession of 'one-off fixers'. The more thoughtful of the professionals themselves recognize that a succession of policies have failed. Thus the architect Michael Fleetwood remarked 'Failure of the free market has made the growth of the State inevitable. But where do we go now the State has failed?'[1] And another very well-known architect, Edward Cullinan, concluded, 'You cannot do local authority housing for long, before you realize that it would be better if you gave them the money instead.'[2] What would this mean in practice? For Rod Hackney it implies 'community architecture'. He explains, 'We as architects, like our clients and political leaders, got it terribly wrong in the 1960s ... Community architecture means attempting to understand the needs of a small group of residents and then working with them and under their instructions and guidance, in order to articulate their case and present it to the various organizations that hold either the purse strings or the approval/rejection powers . . .' This direct responsibility to residents is the role of the professionals in the examples of co-operative housing and self-build that we have examined, and according to David Lawrence, head of GLC professional services, 'there is mounting pressure from an increasing number of London's tenants' groups demanding public money so that they can hire architects to improve their estates.'[3]

Community architecture, thus conceived, has close links with the community politics categorized in Pahl's list of approaches. But what about the 'radical' stance that claims that 'nothing can be solved without changing the whole system'? This is usually argued by Marxists and derives from a well-known dictum of Engels: 'As long as the capitalist mode of production continues to exist it is folly to hope for an isolated settlement of the housing question affecting the lot of the workers. The solution lies in the abolition of the capitalist mode of production and the appropriation of all the means of subsistence and the instruments of labour by the working class itself.'[4] Engels was replying to various forgotten socialists of the kind he labelled as 'utopian' and to disciples of the anarchist Proudhon, who is not forgotten but is certainly unread.

The one thing we all know about Proudhon is his dictum that Property is Theft, – a slogan which, as his biographer remarks, 'was to hang like a verbal albatross around its creator's neck.' George Woodcock explains that

> His boldness of expression was intended for emphasis, and by 'property' he wished to be understood what he later called 'the sum of its abuses'. He was denouncing the property of the man who uses it to exploit the labour of others without any effort on his own part, property distinguished by interest and rent, by the

impositions of the non-producer on the producer. Towards property regarded as 'possession', the right of a man to control his dwelling and the land and tools he needs to live, Proudhon had no hostility; indeed, he regarded it as the cornerstone of liberty, and his main criticism of the Communists was that they wished to destroy it.[5]

With his sympathy with peasants and independent artisans, Proudhon seemed to Marx and Engels to be an absurd survivor from the preindustrial age. Engels declared that '... the ownership of house, garden and field, and security of tenure in the dwelling place, is becoming today, under the rule of large-scale industry, not only the worst hindrance to the worker, but the greatest misfortune for the whole working class, the basis for an unexampled depression of wages below their normal level...'[6]

For most non-Marxists this is an inexplicable point of view which in any case has been bypassed by history. Yet its shadow still haunts the political Left. One modern commentator, wishing to rescue socialism from itself, claims that

> socialists ought to welcome the growth of the home-owning, do-it-yourself sector of production ... the second industrial revolution may be seen as making Marx and Engels wrong about household ownership and production, and Proudhon right about them ... And in practical politics, socialists would no longer have to appear, as they have too often appeared in capitalist and communist countries alike, as enemies of ownership and of free, unalienated domestic productivity – enemies who threaten to confine the working class for ever, no matter how affluent it becomes, to a constricted existence in rented, landless battery housing.[7]

The worst irony is that the dreadful errors of housing

policy were made in times of what now seems like full employment, when levels of investment in the urban fabric were high and when poor people had relatively more disposable income and, consequently, more freedom of manoeuvre than is the case now. In the expansive 1950s our social prophets were urging us to sever, at last, the connection between employment and income. In those days John Kenneth Galbraith was arguing for what he called 'cyclically graduated compensation' – a dole which went up as the economy took a downturn, so that people's purchasing power could be maintained, and which went down when full employment approached. 'One day,' Galbraith forecast, 'we shall remove the economic penalties and also the social stigma associated with involuntary unemployment. This will make the economy much easier to manage.'[8] But, he added, a decade later, 'We haven't done this yet.'

And today, when the collapse of employment for millions makes the need for such policies far more urgent, the political climate is even less receptive to them. Hence the popularity of the Reagan and Thatcher governments among the members of the employed majority who don't feel an obligation to provide an income for those who can't get a job and are never likely to have one. Hence, too, the campaigns against 'social parasites' in the Soviet Union.

André Gorz is a French socialist who warns us that our failure to separate purchasing power from employment is going to lead to a society where the *majority* will be 'marginalized by an unholy alliance of unionized elite workers with managers and capitalists.' And he argues that the political left has been frozen into authoritarian collectivist attitudes belonging to the past:

> As long as the protagonists of socialism continue to make centralized planning (however much it might be broken down into local and regional plans) the linchpin of their programme, and the adherence of

everyone to the 'democratically formulated' objectives of the plan the core of their political doctrine, socialism will remain an unattractive proposition in industrial societies. Classical socialist doctrine finds it difficult to come to terms with political and social pluralism, understood not simply as a plurality of parties and trade unions but as the coexistence of various ways of working, producing and living, various and distinct cultural areas and levels of social existence . . . Yet this kind of pluralism precisely conforms to the lived experience and aspirations of the post-industrial proletariat, as well as the major part of the traditional working class.[9]

How on earth, he asks, has the socialist movement got itself into the position of dismissing as petit-bourgeois individualism all those freedoms which people actually value: everything that belongs to the private niche that people really cherish? He means that niche which can be represented by 'family life, a home of one's own, a back garden, a do-it-yourself workshop, a boat, a country cottage, a collection of antiques, music, gastronomy, sport, love, etc.' And he goes on to assert that 'an inversion of the scale of priorities, involving a subordination of socialized work governed by the economy to activities constituting the sphere of individual autonomy, is under way in every class within the overdeveloped societies and particularly among the post-industrial neo-proletariat.'

It may seem like a bad joke to talk of some of the categories in Gorz's private niche, like that boat, country cottage and collection of antiques, in the context of the new pauper class in Britain. What kind of post-industrial neo-proletariat does he imagine we have, either in Britain or France? But the point he is making is valid enough. With family life, a home of one's own, a back garden, a do-it-yourself workshop, you can get by, as generations of poor people since Proudhon's day have found. David Donnison and Claire Ungerson are wise in their Penguin on *Housing Policy* to reflect on the increasing importance of house and home in a society in which well under half the population is employed outside the home, and in which even employed people spend longer each week at home than at their place of work. They observe that

> Neglect of the domestic economy and the informal economy has led planners, architects and the makers of housing policy under widely different regimes to undervalue space – indoors and outdoors – and the scope which people can be given to extend and adapt their homes and gardens. They have instead been too reluctant to give tenants a stake in their homes or any scope for changing them, and too prone to admire the inflexible, unresponsive bureaucracies which too many housing authorities have made of themselves.[10]

I am sure they are right to envisage a future in which the decline of manufacturing industry as a source of employment is bound to imply a growth in the informal and domestic economy, especially as even the service economy, which was thought capable of taking over the employing function, is being replaced by a self-service economy (e.g. the domestic washing machine taking over from the laundry and even from the launderette). A future where an increasing proportion of goods and services are provided either in the home or the neighbourhood, calls for flexible, adaptable, low-density housing with outdoor as well as indoor space. The once-despised bye-law street of the late nineteenth century as well as the suburban street of the first half of this century, are well adapted to change to accommodate new patterns of living. Modern high-density housing, whether high or low, is not. As the Victorian city, losing population continually and industry disastrously, declines in importance, the chance arises for its adaptation as a low-density city, manageable by its inhabitants. The stumbling block, more than out-of-date notions about the nature of cities, is what Frederick Osborn used to call 'the capitalist plot of land valuation'.

All that derelict urban land is somehow too valuable to be used to the advantage of its citizens. For decades all the institutional investors, insurance companies, pension funds, etc., have put their money in land, and consequently we all have a tacit vested interest in maintaining the pretence that its potential and hypothetical uses as office blocks is more important than its 'uneconomic' use for ordinary human activities. The same phenomenon is observable with rural land. The intractable problem of land valuation underlies our dilemmas over housing, just as it underlies most of the other dilemmas of town and country planning. As Maurice Ash, Chair of the Town and Country Planning Association, puts it,

> Cities have become instruments of oppression because the values generated by their very development have not inhered in their communities, but have disappeared into remote pockets . . . Had those values stayed with the people who generated them, they would have been used to provide their own services; their own schools, their own hospitals, their own parks – instead of, at best, the crumbs that have fallen from local rich men's tables, or the tables of kings, or of what governments or local commissars have imposed. Community is locked in the land, and the key has long since been lost.[11]

It is precisely this that Proudhon meant when he claimed that Property is Theft, and we confuse the matter entirely when we mix it up with the owner-occupier's claim to a few square yards of Britain. But the key issue of land valuation is a political graveyard, as the Labour Party found in its various attempts when in office to cope with it (the 1947 Central Land Board, the 1964 Land Commission and the

Community Land Act of the 1970s). Like the matter of tax relief on mortgage interest, it is an issue too politically sensitive for aspirants for office to feel safe in advocating radical change.

We have, in profusion, analyses of the extent of housing deficiencies from pressure groups like Shelter and from local authority organizations like the AMA, but is it really useful to be told that the country needs to spend £1,000 on repairs and on remedying the shortage for every man, woman and child in the country, when we know that it is not going to be spent? The Labour Party is offering *The Right to a Home*, and the SDP in its green paper, promises *A Choice for All*. Every such document has to be a compromise between interest groups within these parties, and the compilers' assessment of what will win votes.

Political plans for housing have always been dangerously misleading. The numbers game, the propaganda battle of housing start-and-completion statistics, has been played between the two major parties for decades. It was considered a triumph to have achieved the space standards laid down in the wartime Dudley report, and when the Conservatives took over from the postwar Labour government in 1951, Harold Macmillan, the then minister for housing, lowered standards both of space and of construction to achieve a higher propaganda output. I don't mind low space standards at a time when people would prefer a small house to no house, but with one important proviso. Such houses should be so built as to allow for easy and simple enlargement later. This did not happen because the construction systems then adopted did *not* allow for enlargement. Hence, too, the failure of the reasonable notion in private housing of 'starter homes', which were on sites too small for them to be added to. The same political numbers game led to the demand from government for the high-rise system-built housing of the 1960s, with its incredibly expensive legacy of misery.

And it was playing the numbers game that has led to the

continually diminishing attractiveness of large-scale publicly provided housing. Compare Phase One of any estate you know with Phases Two and Three, where, simply at a visual level, all the most attractive features have been pared away by successive economies and are the outward and visible sign of further cuts in initial costs. This is true of the interwar estates, where the early housing, inspired by the work of Raymond Unwin, gave way to the pared-down, mean-spirited borough engineer's version further down the road. It is equally true of postwar housing. Just compare, if you are a Londoner, Phase One of Lillington Street, Pimlico, or Phase One at Thamesmead, with Phase Two in both cases. Housing policy has always been at the whim of every gesture by the Treasury to influence the economy as a whole. At present it is also at the mercy of central government's campaign to take away the residue of local authorities' freedom of decision. The view has grown up among the academics of the Left that council housing is sacred as part of the 'social wage' through which the rich subsidize the poor, but in the lifetime of the present government it has been turned, like so many aspects of social welfare, into a social penalty through which the poor are obliged to subsidize the rich: 'The government has proposed spending targets for local authorities next year which would force many of them to make big profits on their council housing and to use the money to subsidize the rates.'[12] Do we imagine that the officers of the Department of the Environment who have engineered this situation will, in a change of government, surrender this power?

Those who have learned from experience that the only kind of socialism worth considering is that of a self-organizing, self-managing society should not waste their time lobbying the politicians of their choice with a programme for housing which judiciously links every kind of interest group in winning proportions. They should assert that dweller control is the *first* principle of housing, not an optional extra, and should lobby whoever happens to be in power for its extension from the owner-occupation sector to every kind of rented housing, and to the housing of the homeless. We have already reached a situation in London where it would be infinitely cheaper to help homeless families out of pauperization in short-life housing co-ops than to dump them in bed and breakfast hotels. Anne Grosskurth, in her investigation of the thousands of homeless families who face up to three years in bed and breakfast hotels, 'often in appalling conditions', reports,

> There are now over 500 homeless families in B&B from Brent alone, at a cost to the taxpayer in 1982–3 of almost £3 million. If present trends continue, the numbers will more than double over the next two years; by 1986, Brent will be forking out an astronomical £6 million a year to London hoteliers – enough to repair over 21,000 council properties annually. In fact last year's bill was high enough to finance a house-building loan of £100 million to provide permanent housing for every Brent family now in bed and breakfast.[13]

It is easy to see that if a local authority's homeless persons unit is prepared to pay a hotel keeper £100 a week or more to house a homeless family, almost any other form of tenure would be more economical and give more hope and satisfaction to the family itself, and there is a very strong case for giving them the option of forming a short-life co-op, aided by a secondary housing co-operative with an adequate budget for co-operative education work. It's an uphill way out of homelessness but it is a far better one than the perpetuation of total dependency on the decisions of others.

The danger about plans for housing is that, as its term of office ends, the present government will make gestures like the release of funds to local authorities and to the Housing Corporation in response to growing anxiety and anger over the lack of investment in housing, and that this will result in a crash programme to reassure the electors. In such programmes the same assumptions about councils as direct providers of homes will be made, as though there was nothing to learn from the disasters of the past. Similarly the opposition will promise another version of the same plan. When we build again, we need not a plan for housing, but an attitude that will enable millions of people to make their own plans.

Notes

Preface

1. Nick Wates, 'Left-wing Losers', *Architects' Journal*, 1984.
2. Derek Fraser and Anthony Sutcliffe (eds), *The Pursuit of Urban History*, Edward Arnold 1983.

1. Where we went wrong

1. *Suffolk and Essex Free Press*, 17 June 1982.
2. Tony Judge, 'The Political and Administrative Setting' in Hamdi and Greenstreet (eds), *Participation in Housing, No 1: Theory and Implementation*, Oxford Polytechnic Department of Town Planning, Working Paper 57, October 1981.
3. *Suffolk and Essex Free Press*, 17 June 1982.
4. Michael Harloe, 'The Recommodification of Housing' in Harloe and Lebas (eds), *City, Class and Capital*, Arnold 1981.
5. Michael Harloe, 'Towards the Decommodification of Housing? A Comment on Council House Sales', *Critical Social Policy*, Vol. 2, No. 1, Summer 1982.
6. *Observer Business News*, 23 May 1982.
7. *Architects' Journal*, 18 August 1982.
8. Alison Ravetz, *Architects' Journal*, 5 May 1982.
9. Sidney Jacobs, 'Socialist Housing Strategy and Council House Sales', *Critical Social Policy*, Vol. 1, No. 3, Spring 1982.
10. Nicholas John Habraken, *Supports: An Alternative to Mass Housing*, Architectural Press 1972.

11. Staughton Lynd, *Intellectual Origins of American Radicalism*, Pantheon 1968. The first quotation is from Thoreau's *Walden* and the second from Marx's *Economic and Philosophical Manuscripts*; both were written in the 1850s.
12. Norman and Jeanne MacKenzie (eds), *The Diary of Beatrice Webb*, Vol. 1, Virago 1982.
13. Frank Field, *Guardian*, 28 October 1983.

2. Self-help and mutual aid: the stolen vocabulary

1. Sir Milner Holland (Chair), *Report of the Committee on Housing in Greater London*, HMSO 1965.
2. *Illustrated Guide to the New Forest*, Ward Lock 1925.
3. Ferdynand Zweig, *The Worker in an Affluent Society*, Heinemann 1961.
4. S.D. Chapman, 'Working-Class Housing in Nottingham During the Industrial Revolution', *Transactions of the Thoroton Society*, Vol. lxvii, 1963.
5. S.D. Chapman and J.N. Bartlett, 'The Contribution of Building Clubs and the Freehold Land Society to Working-class Housing in Birmingham' in Stanley Chapman (ed.), *The History of Working-Class Housing*, David & Charles 1971.
6. Francis Jones, 'The Aesthetics of the Nineteenth-Century Industrial Town', in H.J. Dyos (ed.), *The Study of Urban History*, Edward Arnold 1968.
7. Elizabeth Ring, *Up the Cockneys*, Elek 1975; Jack Common, *Kiddar's Luck*, Turnstile 1951; Arthur Newton, *Years of Change*, Centreprise 1974; Molly Weir, *Shoes Were for Sundays*, Hutchinson 1970.
8. A.S. Jasper, *A Hoxton Childhood*, Barrie & Rockcliffe 1969, Centreprise 1974.
9. *Architects' Journal*, 17 December 1978.
10. Ivan Illich, *Disabling Professions*, Marion Boyars 1977.
11. Norman Dennis, *People and Planning*, Faber 1970.
12. Ashley Bramall, Leader of the Inner London Education Authority, in *Education*, 3 December 1976.

13. Michael Hughes (ed.), *The Letters of Lewis Mumford and Frederic J. Osborn*, Adams & Dart 1971.
14. Bruce Allsop, *Towards a Humane Architecture*, Frederick Muller 1974.

3. Is selling off a sell-out?

1. Vladimir Voinovich, *The Ivankiad: Or the Tale of the Writer Voinovich's Installation in his New Apartment*, Jonathan Cape 1978.
2. David Donnison and Claire Ungerson, *Housing Policy*, Penguin 1982.
3. J.P. Macey and C.V. Baker, *Housing Management*, second edition, Estates Gazette Ltd 1973.
4. Colin Ward, *Tenants Take Over*, Architectural Press 1974.
5. Alan A. Jackson, *Semi-Detached London*, Allen & Unwin 1973.
6. John Ermisch, *Housing Finance: Who Gains?* Policy Studies Institute, 1–2 Castle Lane, London SW1, 1984.
7. Frank Field, *Do We Need Council Houses?* Catholic Housing Aid Trust 1976.

4. Learning from the poor

1. Chris Birkbeck, 'Garbage, Industry and the "Vultures" of Cali, Colombia' in Ray Bromley and Chris Gerry (eds), *Casual Work and Poverty in Third World Cities*, John Wiley & Sons 1979.
2. *Architectural Design*, August 1963.
3. Janice E. Perlman, *The Myth of Marginality: Urban Poverty and Politics in Rio de Janiero*, University of California Press 1976.
4. *Ibid*.
5. Andrew Hake, *African Metropolis*, Sussex University Press 1977.
6. John F.C. Turner, 'Issues in Self-Help and Self-Managed Housing' in Peter M. Ward (ed.), *Self-Help Housing: A Critique*, Mansell 1982.
7. John F.C. Turner and Robert Fichter (eds), *Freedom to Build*, Collier Macmillan 1972.
8. Turner in P.M. Ward (ed.), *op.cit.* His approach is more

fully described in John F.C. Turner, *Housing By People*, Marion Boyars 1976, available in translation in several languages.
9. Madhu Sarin, 'Urban Planning, Petty Trading and Squatter Settlements in Chandigar, India' in Bromley and Gerry (eds), *op.cit.*, and in a fuller account in Madhu Sarin, *Urban Planning in the Third World*, Mansell 1979.
10. Hans Harms, 'Historical Perspectives on the Practice and Purpose of Self-Help Housing' in Peter M. Ward (ed.), *Self-Help Housing: A Critique*, Mansell 1982.
11. Rod Burgess, 'Self-Help Housing Advocacy: A Curious Form of Radicalism. A Critique of the Work of John F.C. Turner' in Peter M. Ward (ed.), *Self-Help Housing: A Critique*, Mansell 1982.
12. John Gittings, 'Chinese Can Buy Their Own Homes,' *Guardian*, 17 April 1980.
13. F.W. Carter, 'Prague and Sofia: An Analysis of their Changing Internal City Structure' in French and Hamilton (eds), *The Socialist City*, John Wiley & Sons 1979.
14. Denis J.B. Shaw, 'Recreation and the Soviet City' in French and Hamilton, *op.cit.*
15. Jonathan Steele, 'Roumania's Socialism in a Flat Spin', *Guardian*, 6 April 1974.
16. Hugh Stretton, *Urban Planning in Rich and Poor Countries*, Oxford, 1978.
17. Ivan Szelenyi, 'Housing System and Social Structure', *Sociological Review Monograph 17*, 1972.
18. Janos Kenedi, *Do It Yourself: Hungary's Hidden Economy*, Pluto Press 1981.
19. Hugh Stretton, *Capitalism, Socialism and the Environment*, Cambridge University Press 1976.

5. Plots of freedom

1. Walter Southgate, *That's the Way It Was: A Working-Class Autobiography, 1890-1950*, New Clarion Press 1982.
2. Dennis Hardy and Colin Ward, *Arcadia for All: The Legacy of a Makeshift Landscape*, Mansell 1984.
3. Elizabeth Granger, 'A Borrowed Pound', *Bulletin of Environmental Education*, August-September 1976.

4. Jon Gower Davies, *The Evangelizing Bureaucrat*, Tavistock 1972.
5. Colin Jones, *Urban Deprivation and the Inner City*, Croom Helm 1979.
6. Graham Lomas, *The Inner City*, London Council of Social Service 1975.
7. Graham Bennett and Stuart Rutherford, *Architects' Journal*, 31 January 1979.
8. Walter Segal, in an interview with Martin Pawley, *Architects' Journal*, 20 June 1984.
9. Walter Segal, *RIBA Journal*, July 1977.
10. *Architects' Journal*, 17 December 1980.
11. *Ibid.*
12. Walter Segal, speaking at the RIBA, 2 March 1982.
13. Ken Atkins in *Bulletin of Environmental Education*, October 1983.
14. Walter Segal, 'View from a lifetime', *Transactions of the RIBA*, Vol. 1, 1982.
15. 'Self-build Home Scheme Planned for Stirling', *Scotsman*, 30 March 1984.

6. Rediscovering co-operation

1. *Councils and their Tenants*, Political and Economic Planning 1948.
2. Stanley Alderson, *Britain in the Sixties: Housing*, Penguin 1962.
3. Alison Ravetz, 'Nasty, Brutish and Short', *Architects' Journal*, 5 May 1982.
4. 'World in Action', ITV 19 March 1984.
5. Harold Campbell, *Housing: a Co-operative Approach*, Co-operative Union 1959.
6. Harold Campbell in *Roof*, May 1979.
7. Tony Gibson, Introduction to Peter Stead, *Local Initiatives in Great Britain*, Vol. III, *Housing*, New Foundations 1982.
8. Tom Clay, 'The Liverpool Co-ops', *Architects' Journal*, 5 July 1978.
9. Solon Co-operative Housing Services Ltd, Annual Report 1983–1984.

10. Nick Wates, 'The Liverpool Breakthrough: or Public Sector Housing Phase 2', *Architects' Journal*, 8 September 1982.
11. Hugh Anderson, 'Co-op Dividends', *Architects' Journal*, 18 July 1984.
12. Jeremy Seabrook, *The Idea of Neighbourhood: What Local Politics Should Be About*, Pluto Press 1984.
13. Jane Morton, 'Tenant Takeover', *New Society*, 16 June 1983.
14. Jane Morton, 'Glasgow's Socialist Co-ops', *New Society*, 10 May 1984.
15. Tony Gibson, *Counterweight: The Neighbourhood Option*, Town and Country Planning Association 1984.
16. 'Co-ops Plan for Troubled Liverpool Estates', *Guardian*, 3 May 1983.
17. 'Housing Co-ops Fight Labour Council Coup', *Guardian*, 15 August 1983.
18. Jules Lubbock, 'Housing for Need', *New Statesman*, 14 October 1983.

7. Leavening the Lump

1. See the detailed survey of the extent of tenant investment in David A. Kirby, 'The Maintenance of Prewar Council Dwellings', *Journal of the Institution of Municipal Engineers*, May 1972.
2. Richard Bourne and Jessica Gould, *Self-Sufficiency 16–25*, Kogan Page 1983.
3. John Tilley, *Changing Prospects for Direct Labour*, Fabian Society 1976.
4. Tom Forester, 'Direct Labour – New Moves', *New Society*, 11 November 1976.
5. Jon Bright and Geraldine Petterson, *The Safe Neighbourhoods Unit*, Section 4, 'Operational Difficulties', NACRO 1984.
6. Dave Lamb, *The Lump: an Heretical Analysis*, Solidarity 1974.
7. Dave Lamb, letter to *New Society*, 3 April 1975.
8. Anthony Mason, *Worker Motivation in Building*, Institute of Building 1979.

9. See Seymour Melman, *Decision-making and Productivity*, Blackwell 1968.
10. David Douglass, *Pit Life in Durham*, History Workshop 1972.
11. See Appendix III, 'Building Co-ops' in Colin Ward, *Tenants Take Over*, Architectural Press 1974.
12. For comments on the rise and fall of Sunderlandia by one of its founders see Robert Oakshott, *The Case for Workers' Co-ops*, Routledge & Kegan Paul 1978.
13. Interview in *Your own Boss?*, Krow Books 1978.
14. R.E. Pahl, 'Deindustrialization and Social Polarization', *Work and Society Newsletter* April 1984. See his *Divisions of Labour*, Blackwell 1984.
15. Jonathan Bradshaw, 'Disincentives to Working in the Benefit System', *Work and Society Newsletter*, April 1984.

8. Do we need a plan?

1. Michael Fleetwood, *Architects' Journal*, 21 April 1982.
2. Edward Cullinan, *Voices*, Channel 4, May 1984.
3. *Architects' Journal*, 6 July 1983.
4. Frederick Engels, *The Housing Question*, Lawrence & Wishart 1940.
5. George Woodcock, Introduction to P.-J. Proudhon, *What is Property?*, Dover Publications 1970.
6. Engels, *op.cit.*
7. Hugh Stretton, *Urban Planning in Rich and Poor Countries*, Oxford 1978.
8. John Kenneth Galbraith, *The Affluent Society*, Hamish Hamilton 1958.
9. André Gorz, *Farewell to the Working Class: an Essay on Post-industrial Socialism*, Pluto Press 1983.
10. David Donnison and Clare Ungerson, *Housing Policy*, Penguin 1982.
11. Maurice Ash, 'Towns, Tongues and Taxes', *Town and Country Planning*, September 1984.
12. 'Council Tenants to Subsidize the Rates', *Guardian*, 3 August 1984.
13. Anne Grosskurth, 'When Home is a B&B Hotel', *Roof*, January/February 1984.